Who shares your problem?

Neil Henson

Who shares your problem?

or

How to succeed using a
Partnership Problem Solving
Process, at both Strategic and
Practitioner levels

Neil Henson
Sixth Sense Training Limited
Berkshire UK

Produced by Butler Systems Design Limited www.butlersystems.com

ISBN - 13:978-1470050146

Version 1.2

Contents

About the author

Neil Henson has been working as a Problem Solving Advisor and Trainer in Problem Solving and Partnership Working since 1998. He has been employed all across the UK and in parts of the USA in both the Corporate and Public Sectors.

In 2001 he received a London Metropolitan Police Commendation for Problem Solving for a £2 Million multi agency project. He was subsequently credited in the "Crime Opportunity Profiling of Streets" report in 2005. In 2003 he was the winner of the UK Home Office Tilley Award for Organisational Support for Problem Solving. In 2006 he received a Metropolitan Police Commendation for Mainstreaming Problem Solving and Partnership Working across London, UK.

Neil has been a judge for Problem Solving for the UK Home Office in 2004, Hampshire Police and London Metropolitan Police 2005 and 2006. In 2006 he was made an Honorary Kentucky Colonel for contributions to Problem Solving.

Neil was credited by the UK Local Government Improvement and Development in 2009 and the Office of Community Oriented Policing US Dept of Justice.

Neil has been a speaker at the UK Problem Oriented Partnership Conferences 2003, 2004 and 2009, the International Problem Oriented Police Conferences 2003 and 2005; the Kentucky Chiefs of Police Convention in 2008 and the Scottish Community Safety Conference in 2010. He was a facilitator at the Nordic Problem Solving Symposium 2006; the Scottish Borders Community Safety Conference 2011, the Scottish Railways Conference 2011, Surrey Neighbourhood Police Conference 2012 and the UK Neighbourhood Policing Conference 2012.

Introduction

I am obsessed with Problem Solving. You might as well know that right now. I can't switch off and, like most things, there are advantages and disadvantages. I keep identifying problems and coming up with ways to solve them but unfortunately can't keep them to myself! The advantage for you is that this book provides you with the clarity to take on problems with others. It contains really useful material adapted from other professions and is supported with lots of examples.

There are many definitions of Problem Solving, and this is mine.

Problem Solving is changing the current situation into something better, and keeping it that way.

To change your situation into something better, it helps if you are proficient in using the different elements of Problem Solving, have the skills to successfully apply them and the intrinsic motivation to keep going when things are working against you.

This book on Problem Solving takes you through all the fundamentals including how to define your problem because, unless you get that right, all the following actions are wasted or even counterproductive. It will also explain how to do your own research, how to be inspired by others to create your own ways of doing something and how to measure what you have done to see if it worked. The skills covered in the book include how to write reports that focus on the problem and possible solutions, how to manage your Problem Solving Meetings and how to deliver presentations.

To assist practitioners, a number of Problem Solving Processes have been written over the years. These are really helpful as they guide the practitioner through the interrelated tasks. I have my own, called PARTNERS, which underpins each chapter, as you will find throughout the book.

Finally, I know that you can work on problems in isolation, but it is much better to work with others who also suffer the consequences of the problems. These are described as Partners and to find yours is to ask yourself the question, "Who shares my problem?"

PARTNERS: A Problem Solving Process

As you will see, the structure of this book takes you through each stage of a Problem Solving Process. I have created the mnemonic, PARTNERS to enable you to recall the different stages and to remind you to seek out those who share your problem, your partners.

The process has been designed to be user-friendly and has captured good practice from both the Corporate and Public sectors. It has been designed to encourage creative responses to problems while working within a framework based upon well-researched evidence and analysis. This process and supporting paperwork can be found on our website www.sixthsensetraining.co.uk

P	Problem and Partner Identification
A	Aim Setting
R	Research and Analysis
T	Thinking Creatively
N	Negotiating the Changes
E	Evaluation
R	Recognition and Reward
S	Sharing 'Good Practice'

Who shares your problem?

Chapter 1

Problem Definition and Partner Identification

The purpose of this chapter is to help you:

A - Define your problem clearly

B - Identify your partners

Partnership Problem Solving Process	
P	**Problem and Partner Identification**
A	Aim Setting
R	Research and Analysis
T	Thinking Creatively
N	Negotiating the Changes
E	Evaluation
R	Recognition and Reward
S	Sharing 'Good Practice'

Chapter 1

Part A - Defining your problem and how to recognise a poor definition.

Introduction

A resident of a village was concerned about motorists speeding through it, and asked for a 'speed camera' to slow down the motorists as they entered the village. His request was turned down. So instead he constructed a bird box and placed it in his garden. The box just by coincidence was painted yellow set on an 8 foot high pole on the edge of his garden, which just happened to be the first thing motorists saw when entering the village. The cars entering the village slowed down.

When you face a problem, you will normally want to solve it and move on to the next pressing issue. However, you need to be clear about what you are actually trying to solve. This section will help you define the problem and recognise a poorly defined one. This is important as the problem you are working on may have been given to you to resolve, especially if you have a reputation for getting things done, and you need to make sure that what you have been tasked to do is in fact achievable.

Defining your problem

Defining the problem accurately is the keystone of Problem Solving. Define it incorrectly and all subsequent work could be aimed at the wrong set of 'goalposts'.

A well-defined problem can usually be recorded in one sentence, but be prepared for it to take a long time to get it right. If it is two or more paragraphs, you are likely to have more than one problem or you do not know what it is. To give you a general guide it normally takes between 14 and 20 words to describe one problem clearly.

Expect to go back and redefine your problem when you know more about it. This normally comes about when you have undertaken your research, or after you have put in different actions and studied the results.

Two types of problems

I have seen a number of ways that problems have been described. I see two types of problems, those having just one cause or those that are made up of a number of factors which, when combined, create the problem.

One cause

For example, if your vacuum cleaner is not picking up the dirt from the floor, then it is going to be a single problem and, from my experience, it's normally the part most difficult to access that has come loose!

Multiple causes

For other problems there are a number of factors, some worse than others, that when combined create a problem. For example, we are suffering the decline of all types of bees. There are many theories for this. The factors believed to be causing the decline are insecticides, herbicides, infections, spread of diseases, predators etc. No one is sure of the cause but most believe it is a combination of all the factors.

Types of poorly defined problems

Over the years, on examining problems, I have found that there are eight common mistakes that people make when defining their problems.

1 - Multiple problems	5 - Limited description
2 - Consequences	6 - It is just a statement
3 - Too much jargon	7 - Implied cause
4 - Not being clear	8 - Aspirational

1 - Multiple problems

If you can't describe your problem in a single sentence, you've probably got more than one problem. This is the most recurring difficulty with problems I see as a Problem Solving Advisor. There could be many problems taking place and for convenience they are all grouped together, for no other reason than that they share the same location or result.

For example, 'Everyone is late for the conference'. You must separate the problems here, as there may be a number of different reasons why people are late for the conference. It could be poor directions from the train station, not enough cabs or not enough parking spaces. You need to identify each one, set an aim for each one and then prioritise which of the problems need to be worked on first. It maybe that one problem is accounting for the majority of the people being late. Once you have identified the problem you need to find others to work with who share your problem. For example, another organiser may have the same problem of people being late.

You will also have to look at the true reasons why people are late, and not just the ones they are offering up as excuses. It maybe that some are intentionally turning up late, as they never like the opening sessions of conferences, which means that whatever you do will not make a difference.

Only when you have identified all the problems can you have the option of grouping them under a broader Strategic Aim. The benefit of this is that it will make it easier to coordinate the separate problems with the respective partners and actions.

For example, you may be responsible for a shopping centre that has a decline in people coming to it. The Strategic Aim could be "To increase the prosperity of the ABC Shopping centre by X % by a specific date". The problems which at present are working against your Strategic Aim could be high levels of traffic congestion; too many empty stores or that your main store, known as an anchor store as it holds others in place, is threatening to withdraw. Each of these problems is likely to have a different partner, time scale and probably different funding available.

2 - Consequences

This is where you have described the consequences or symptoms of the problem, rather than the problem itself.

For example, if you described the problem as "Injuries from broken bottles", as opposed to "The sale of alcohol to under-aged youths, resulting in drunk and disorderly behaviour and assaults."

If you and your partnership only have the capability to tackle the consequences, then acknowledge that's what you're doing and select the most applicable response from the Impact Scale. The Impact Scale gives you more choices when setting an aim and is covered in Chapter 2.

Just as an aside, having looked at this problem, there were many reasons: easy access to bottles; people becoming violent when drunk; and even people fighting those who they believed had jumped the queue at a kebab shop. Another contributing factor was that minicab firms, faced with assaults themselves, reduced the times they worked in the city centre making it more difficult for people to get home. Consequently, fights sometimes occurred between individuals within the groups of people who were roaming the town looking for cabs.

As you can see, even the decline of minicabs was not the problem, but the consequence of the actual problems of the assaults and fare evasions. To end on a positive note, this was addressed by Ayr Community Safety Partnership, Western Scotland. They resolved it with a partnership between all interested parties. One measure was the employment of Taxi Marshalls. These people oversaw the whole process and as a result, assaults and fare evasions went down, which in turn encouraged more mini cabs, which meant fewer drunken people wandering around the town. It was also self sustaining, because a fee was added to the fare which, in turn, funded the Taxi Marshalls.

3 - Too much jargon

The use of acronyms is exclusionary and most organisations have their own jargon which means nothing to people from other organisations. This isn't an issue until you want to involve other partners. Then it can be one of the biggest stumbling blocks to working together and making sense of information. Do you want to have to employ an interpreter for every meeting? If in doubt, explain an acronym or even better, get rid of it.

4 - Not being clear

This is different from jargon. Unfortunately, it's been my experience that some people have not understood the problem and not had the confidence to say so. They then mask this with terminology that sounds knowledgeable but doesn't stand up to scrutiny. Therefore, clarity is all important if you want people to understand the precise nature of the problem.

Plain English should always be used when recording your problem, which can be defined as that which "any reasonable person can understand after only one reading" (Steve Colgan). The main advantages of Plain English is that it is faster to read and enables you to get your message across more often, more easily and in a friendlier way.

Just like the use of jargon, if you are going to write in a way that is not Plain English, you are going to make it difficult for your partners to work with you, as they will not know what your actual problem is. Also, when trying to generate ideas, being unclear about the problem will not help people to think of different ways to resolve it.

5 - Limited description

This is the opposite problem of people writing too much. This is when they write just two or three words and expect the reader to know exactly what they mean. I am a supporter of brevity, but if you write just a couple of words you make it unnecessarily difficult for others to appreciate the problem and therefore they cannot help you.

6 - It is just a statement

This is where what you've recorded is a statement rather than a problem.

One method to test whether the problem has been described as a statement is to ask questions such as "So why is that a problem?" or "So what?"

To ask "So what?" is a very powerful method to draw out the exact problem, but can be misinterpreted as not caring.

For example "Cars driving up and down the sea front at night." So what? It's better to isolate specific problems being caused e.g. "Cars being raced recklessly causing danger to pedestrians."

7 - Implied cause

This is where a person has added, though not directly, what they believe to be the cause into their definition.

For example, have a look at this definition. "We are suffering from a reduction in sales due to the recession." You have to ask if they are basing their definition on what they know, or what they believe? The difficulty of putting an implied cause into your problem definition is that you risk overlooking other factors that are contributing to your problem.

In this case it might not be that people are not spending money but that they are spending it on other things or with your competitors. Also, it might be the attitude and behaviour of the sales team that is actually causing the decline in sales. In that case, the company will need to invest time and resources looking at this area.

8 - Aspirational

This is where someone records the aim without defining the problem. For example, "We want more people to come into the town centre at night", as opposed to identifying the reasons why people don't come and, for those that do come, why they don't come more often. To get to the problem(s) you have to work back one stage and find out why the numbers coming in to the town centre are reducing. You will also need to put the decline into context. Does this happen often at this time of year, is it happening to other town centres and is this a year on year trend.

Although writing an aim when you are trying to describe the Problem is a mistake, the definition of your aim, beginning with the word "How" is a great way to open a session dedicated to generating ideas. For example, "How can we get more people to come to the town centre at night?"

We will look at creating ideas later in the book.

Part B - Finding partners who share your problems and aims. Working with reluctant partners.

Introduction

When you work on a problem, you are likely to immerse yourself into it. This is understandable but you could be missing opportunities to work with others on resolving the problem. These people, organisations or even pressure groups could have expertise in the field or have access to a greater network and would benefit from your success. These people are best described as partners.

Your partners

One way to see if they could be a partner, you need to ask yourself this question, **"Do they share my problem?"** If they do share your problem, they are likely to be a partner. The obvious ones will come to mind easily, but there are others who will take more time to find.

Therefore, when faced with a problem, look at who else is dealing with it or the consequences of it. You may find them on site visits to the problem; as a result of meetings called to address the problem or from your own research. Each time please ask yourself "Do they share my problem?" If "yes", then work to include them in your partnership.

A definition of a partnership

A partnership is an agreement, formal or informal, made between people, groups or organisations where they have agreed to cooperate, sometimes just for a set period of time, to progress a **shared aim or purpose.**

A partnership with a shared problem

Here is an example of a problem which, when you look at in depth, shows just how many partners are involved. You may equally have a large number of partners who actually share your problem.

During the first six months of 2002, there were 91 reported vehicle arsons in a London Borough. Ten of those offences occurred in just one road and a further 15 fires were in a nearby industrial estate. Each fire was estimated to have cost thousands in the emergency services response, removal and destruction of the burnt vehicles and road repairs.

As the problem affected a number of partners, a group of people was put together with the specific purpose of reducing car fires. Consultation with the Fire and Rescue Service revealed that they expected a significant rise in the number of vehicle arsons during the school summer holidays.

Further research identified that the arson attacks were aimed at low value vehicles that had apparently been abandoned at the above sites. The trigger factor to these attacks appeared to be the affixing of a notice to the vehicles indicating that the local authority would remove them after two weeks. This problem was resolved with a change in procedure.

Together with the fire service and the local authority, a protocol was devised which removed target vehicles within 24 hrs.

The result was that vehicle arsons at the above sites were eliminated. Just as an aside, the problem was not just displaced. In fact, the surrounding area benefitted by a 57% reduction in vehicle arson.

These are some of the people who shared the problem and why.

Residents in the road
It was worrying to have cars set on fire. They feared that their own car would be set on fire and that the car fires would spread. A burnt out car takes up at least one parking space. It would not be good if they were trying to sell their house.

Businesses on the Industrial Site
Virtually the same as the residents but also it may encourage the setting on fire of other properties, as well as putting off potential employees.

Council Rate payers
It costs about £5,000 per car, including the cost of towing away the car and the repair of the road surface.

Highways Department
The cost of repairing the road surface comes from their budget which means that other repairs could not be undertaken.

Community Safety Team
They have the lead for reducing anti social behaviour and crime.

London Fire and Rescue
Their crews are called out to deal with car fires which are dangerous. The danger is not only from the chance of explosion of the fuel, but also from the brake fluid which, when heated, becomes an acid which burns through the protective clothing of the fire-fighters causing severe injuries.

Metropolitan Police

They have a responsibility to reduce anti social behaviour and crime and have to investigate the crime. This involves detectives' investigative time to find the offender and the costs of sending material for forensic examination.

You can see from this example just how many people are involved in the one problem of the cars being set on fire.

Do they share your aim?

Another way to find partners is to seek others who share the same aims, if not the problems. It maybe that you are an industry trying to open up new trading areas and that you could find another business that wants to do the same, but which does not compete with yours. Sometimes their aims or aspirations are recorded in documents that you can have access to. Having a mutual or shared aim would be a good basis for opening up a conversation with them.

A partnership with a shared aim

In the 1990's lobster catches declined off the coast of Cornwall UK. There were a number of theories as to the reason and many people were involved in the problem. The belief held by some was that it was the result of overfishing by the local fisherman and that their catches should be limited or stopped completely. However, the Cornish fishing fleets had been in decline for two decades and so this assumption was wrong.

Here are some of the reasons for the decline in lobsters.

There had been changes to the marine environment through pollution. British people like eating cod and lots of it, eating one-third of all the cod consumed in the world and 85% of cod caught in European waters. As cod stocks had been declining due to over-fishing, smaller fish like herring had increased. At the same time, the British people were not eating as much herring as they had before. This was unfortunate for the lobsters because herring like eating young lobsters.

So who shares the problem of declining lobster stocks?

We can take it as given that the lobsters share the problem. Here are some of the others.

The fisherman and the National Federation of Fisheries Organisations (NFFO) and the Cornwall Sea Fisheries Committee

The environmentalist groups such as Greenpeace and Worldwide Fund for Nature (WWF)

Government departments for Fishing

Local restaurateurs and their customers

All these groups set aside any differences and worked together to change the circumstances to one they all preferred, an increase in lobster stocks.

What has been done?

Firstly, the female lobsters carrying eggs, normally returned to the sea by fishermen, are now passed on to a newly created local National Lobster Hatchery which is funded by charitable donations, business partners and Cornish District Councils.

The larvae develop in this protected environment and, when they are large enough, are released back into the sea where they can resist the herring. The hatchery itself has become a tourist attraction and is therefore more likely to be a sustainable action.

Has it worked?

Yes, there has been an increase in fishermens' catches in that there is an increased number of young lobsters present along the coast.

Ways to present your problem to others

At some point you are going to need to brief others about the problem, and it is always good to have material already prepared for additional opportunities. Here are some ways that this could be done.

Write a report

You can present it as a written report. A way to write a report can be found in Appendix 3.

Produce a DVD

You could use a DVD to present the problem. Although it does take time in writing the script, visiting the problem to film it and recording interviews of people affected, it is a very powerful medium. I do recommend employing a specialist for the voice over.

Presentation

You could present the problem as a formal presentation. How to conduct a problem oriented presentation is covered in Appendix 4.

Discussion

You could deliver it as an informal discussion and seek out the opinions and observations of others.

People who do not share your problem or aim

Have you ever been working on a problem or a project and found that some people were either not doing what had been agreed, or they were not doing as much as you had expected them to do?

It could be that they just do not share your problem. It took me a while to realise that people either share your problem or they don't. Then it is a matter of whether you want to encourage the person to share it or accept that they won't.

There may even be people and organisations that actually benefit from your problem. They may have the contract to sort things out, manage the consequences or their funding depends on its existence.

If we go back to the problem of the car fires, then the person who had the contract for towing away the burnt out cars is someone who may not welcome a lack of work. Equally, the company who was contracted to repair the road surface would have welcomed the regular work.

How to encourage others to share your problem

There are going to be situations where others need to make more of a contribution to resolving a problem. These occur in most industries but, for a really good range of methods, let us look at the world of law enforcement.

Those in law enforcement have problems which need others to play their part in making improvements to the situation but, for a number of reasons, those people do not help out.

The following advice has been adapted from a document called: Shifting and Sharing Responsibility for Public Safety Problems - Community Oriented Policing Services by Herman Goldstein and Michael S Scott (2005). – US Department of Justice, Office of Community Oriented Policing Services. Response Guide No.3. Available for free download from the Center for Problem Oriented Policing website www.popcenter.org

Have a look and see how many of these approaches you recognise and how many you could use for your situation. You may want to see how many of these methods have been used against you.

1. Educate others regarding their responsibility for the problem.

This is when you take time to get others to accept their responsibility for the problem. They may not even be aware of the consequence of what they are doing.

For example, there is concern about the considerable loss of other species by the Tuna Fishing Industry using certain fishing methods. Therefore, environmentalist groups have approached the large retailers to explain to them the consequences of buying fish caught using certain methods. As a result, the majority of the retailers now only buy tuna that has been caught by the pole and line method and not by large indiscriminate nets.

2. Make a straightforward, informal request for someone to assume responsibility for the problem.

This is when you approach the person or organisation to do something about the fact that they are causing the problem.

For example, some telephone marketing companies employ 'predictive dialling', a computerised system which systematically dials telephone numbers of potential customers. The aim is that when the call is answered, the person receiving the call is connected to someone from their sales department. However, if all the staff are busy, then instead of the call being put through, it is terminated, or worse still, the line is left open with the receiver hearing nothing. This proves very disturbing for those receiving the calls. As a result of an approach made by an overseeing body, a voluntary code of conduct has been adopted for the industry.

3. Make a targeted, confrontational request to assume responsibility for the problem.

This is when you use a more direct approach to a person or organisation, probably due to the fact that earlier efforts were unsuccessful.

For example, in the clothing manufacturing industry, if a pressure group working against child labour, identifies a company whose suppliers are breaching regulations regarding their workforce, they focus on that specific company and make their point, sometimes with publicity events. The company is normally a sub contractor, but the response from the leading branded company is swift to address the problem.

4. Engage another existing organisation that has the capacity to help address the problem.

This is when entering into a Partnership with another will be beneficial to all those involved. Whether you have different problems but a shared aim, or you have the same problem but different aims, as long as everyone is clear about what they want and there is no conflict of interests, then they can engage together.

For example, you may have had trouble with a builder. Your aim is to have your extension completed and your home habitable. A Television Company is looking to run a series on how they can expose rogue builders, redress the poor building work and create a home which prompts the owner to be both emotional and grateful. You would have to be engaged by the TV Company to feature your home and the TV Company needs to be engaged by you to enable the cameras to be present.

5. Press for the creation of a new organisation to assume responsibility for the problem.

This is going to be when a Partnership is created for the sole purpose of addressing the problems and meeting the aims of all those involved.

For example the Federation against Copyright Theft (FACT) was established in 1983. Its primary purpose is to protect the United Kingdom's film and broadcasting industry against counterfeiting and copyright and trademark infringements.

6. Shame the delinquent organisation, person or department by calling public attention to its failure to assume responsibility for the problem.

This is when a person or organisation is approached by others in a confrontational style. There is very little room for a "win win" result here and by cornering another party you may risk a counter attack, whereby they equally shame you. Therefore, if you are going to use this option please make sure you are ready for the response. I mention this as people may not welcome being named and shamed and, instead of appreciating the feedback, they may think "Right, I'll get you back for that!" Also, you need to consider that a short term gain may have a detrimental impact on the development of a long term relationship.

7. Withdraw services relating to certain aspects of the problem.

This is when a person or organisation reaches the point when they no longer wish to manage the consequences of another's choices.

For example, buildings which have a high number of false alarms and make no genuine efforts to address the problem get placed on a list of properties to which the police no longer respond.

8. Charge fees for services related to the problem.

This is when a person or organisation literally penalises another for failing to do anything, or anything worthwhile, to reduce the problem.

For example, some Fire and Rescue departments charge others for their services, though there is always a tension between maintaining goodwill and making someone improve the situation. Wiltshire UK Fire and Rescue Department charged someone for removing a trapped bird from a chimney. At first, this seems a bit harsh until you know that they had been to the same address on an earlier occasion for exactly the same problem and the occupier had failed to take their advice to fit a cover over the top of the chimney.

9. Press for legislation mandating that measures are taken to prevent the problem.

This is when a person or organisation employs the Law to get another to do something about a recurring problem.

For example, as a result of the Great Fire of London, which started on 2 September 1666, it was soon clear that the wooden construction of London's buildings had added greatly to the spread of the fire. As a result, King Charles II issued a proclamation saying that all buildings were to be built out of stone and roads were to be widened.

The English Government looked at legislation and introduced laws aimed specifically at fire prevention. The **London Cooking Fire Bylaw 1705,** specifically prohibited open fires in the attics of thatched buildings.

10.**Bring a civil action to compel another organisation, person department to accept responsibility for the problem.**

This is an alternative to employing legislation, as mentioned in the previous example. This is when people take their dispute through the Civil Courts, where the burden of proof required is less than in a criminal court.

Employ the tactics together as a Partnership

Maybe you have employed these methods or variations in the past or have even been at the receiving end. Normally, if you are going to employ any of these options, see if it could be a joint action with other partners. A number of organisations working together can only strengthen the case, as it shows that it is not just one person being vindictive or confrontational to another.

Summary

You have defined your problem and looked at people who could work with you, best described as your partners. I recognise that working in a partnership is hard work but the benefits are worth it. You now need to clarify what you want to achieve. The next chapter, therefore, will look at setting an aim.

Who shares your problem?

Chapter 2

Setting your Aim

The purpose of this chapter is to help you:

Write an effective aim and recognise a poorly written one

Have alternatives when setting an aim

Partnership Problem Solving Process	
P	Problem and Partner Identification
A	**Aim Setting**
R	Research and Analysis
T	Thinking Creatively
N	Negotiating the Changes
E	Evaluation
R	Recognition and Reward
S	Sharing 'Good Practice'

Chapter 2

Setting your Aim

Introduction

Now that you have defined your problem and found your partners you will need to decide what you want to do: the Aim. This needs to be clearly defined, be capable of being measured and have an end date. If this is not done you will not know when you have done enough or when you need to make an assessment of whether what you are doing is working.

Do not be pressurised to act

After looking at the problem, you naturally move towards doing something about it and this will, in turn, become the aim. You will need to consider so many factors when setting your aim, including the target and timescale. However, there can be a real threat to setting a realistic target and timescale if external pressure forces you to start your actions far too early. This undue pressure is going to: limit your ability to think; risk you making poor judgements; put a strain on your working relationships with your partners and have a detrimental effect on the capacity of your team.

In fact, intense pressure to do something normally just triggers off activity with the intention of placating those making the demand to have something done, or those acting on the behalf of others affected by the problem. This means that those tasked with working on the problem have to spend their time and resources on undertaking the activity.

Not only is this wasteful, it severely reduces opportunities for people to think of alternative ways of doing something.

However, you do have two other choices, do nothing or just monitor the situation.

Do nothing

I spend a lot of my time visiting problems and speaking to people. Most of the people I meet have a commendable work ethic but are really stressed. With these people in mind, I prioritise the next three points.

Point 1: Just because someone tells you it is a problem does not necessarily make it so.

Point 2: Just because someone has chosen to tell you, it does not mean you have to do something about it.

Point 3: Just because you are the lead, does not mean that you have to do something immediately.

I make these points to get them to reflect on what they are doing and, equally important, how they are feeling. The competing demands to deal with problems make them feel stressed and, from my experience, people under pressure do not always make the best decisions. Therefore, when people present a problem to you, you do have the option of not reacting but of considering the three points and to think of who else could be better placed to take the lead.

Monitor the situation

The second option is that you just watch and wait. Others may not be comfortable with that approach so you will have to state that you are monitoring the situation and resist the pressure to act. There may be times when you could make the situation worse if you do not have the chance to appreciate the dynamics of what is going on.

For example, during the Vietnam War a military outpost had a problem of snakes. Before their presence was appreciated, the snakes were exterminated. Unfortunately for the troops stationed at the outpost, the snakes were there having been drawn to the growing rat population and, once the snakes were removed, the rat population exploded resulting in the post having to be abandoned.

It may be that a series of events had combined to cause the problem, ones which were unlikely to occur again. Your actions, therefore, would be wasted. Or you may just not have the time, people or resources to make a difference to the problem, however keen you are to get started.

What is it you want to achieve?

There is going to be a need to set a clear aim and there is a widely known mnemonic called SMART to guide the person. There are many variations of SMART. Here is the one I prefer.

S - Specific

Make sure the aim "hits the nail on the head." For example, a company may set an aim to increase profits, by a certain percentage, by a set time.

M - Measurable

Make sure that you know whether you've achieved your aim. Decide on effective ways to measure success. For example, you could measure the number of people satisfied with your cashiers, based on previous research that showed the satisfaction rate was 60%.

A - Achievable

This is to make sure that you set a realistic target. This target will be influenced by the time scale and the resources and expertise available. Later in this chapter we will look at choices that are available to ensure your aim is achievable, described as the Impact Scale.

R - Relevant

Does your Objective and Action plan work towards meeting your targets and your overall strategy? Sometimes the action is a good one, just not the one needed to achieve your aim.

T - Time-framed

Set realistic timescales for completion of your plan and for regular monitoring along the way. It will need an end date and not just something like six months, because when you read it at a later date it will still read "six months". It is far better to set an actual date, including the day, such as 31 March (then the year).

Mistakes people make when setting their aim

There are mistakes that can occur when setting an aim. Here are some of the most common ones I have found.

Recording an action into the aim

All too frequently people include an action within the aim. For example, "We need to increase sales of our book by 10% by a set date by undertaking more presentations at conferences."

The aim should be "To increase the sales by 10% by the set date." and not include the action regarding the presentations. Even though the action is valid as a method, it is just one of a number of actions that could be done to increase sales of the book and, if just one action is included in the aim, then it could exclude all the other choices. For example, book sales could be increased by creating a link to Amazon on your own website.

Making the aim too broad

Sometimes people set an aim which is too vague. This means either the real problem is not worked on or resources are spread too thinly. This is best described in the expression, "if you defend everything you defend nothing." It is therefore better to be more specific and have recognised stages with specific partners, than to move without clear direction.

Setting people up to fail

Although earlier we talked about setting an achievable aim, there is an argument that setting a far reaching target energises the group to excel and great results are achieved. These are known as 'Stretch Objectives'. These stretched objectives are seen as generating more creative ideas and enhanced team working. However, if they're stretched too far, people will not bother at all as they will be seen as unachievable.

No end date

This is when the aim is written but has no end date. This means the initiative could just keep going without a time when it is looked at to decide whether to change the actions, or to end them.

Working with partners

Do you share the same aim?

There can be another opportunity to find others with whom you could work with as partners, when you set your aim. You may not have found them when you asked yourself, "Who shares my problem?" but you may find your partners by asking yourself the question, "Who shares my aim?"

For example, underage drinking can lead to anti social behaviour, with the lead on this problem taken by the local police and local government. At the same time some of the young people, while intoxicated, take part in unprotected sex. This in turn leads to an increase in sexually transmitted diseases, with the lead being local Health providers. The same unprotected sex can lead to underage pregnancies. Again the lead would be the Health Authorities but also the Education Department who have an obligation to provide education to the mother. Therefore, other interventions would have to be put in place to provide classrooms with child care facilities. As you can see, the problem and its consequences involve a number of people who share the same aim, which is the reduction in the number of occasions where young people become drunk.

Problems caused to other partners

The question you will need to consider is whether achieving your aim will have a detrimental effect on your partners. If so, is there a way it could be achieved without causing them a problem. It may be that no other choice is available, so at least tell them that it is going to be applied, so they are ready to respond. For example, prisons routinely release prisoners on a Friday, if the actual date of their release falls on a Saturday or Sunday. This means an increase of demand on the Probation Service and those providing accommodation, on probably the worst day of the week to get anything done.

Another situation that causes problems for other partners is when one agency promises something on behalf of another partner that they cannot deliver, such as suggesting an action that is logistically really difficult or is legally not possible to do.

Does it match your partner's values?

It may be that your aim goes against their values. In that case, they may have to abstain from this aim or even work against you. But, as long as you are up front about it, your partnership can survive these differences.

What is really an achievable aim?

Earlier we looked at the frequently used SMART aim and one part states that the aim must be achievable. The difficulty is deciding on what is really achievable. You may not get help from those making the demand, as they invariably want the problem to go completely. Fortunately, something has been devised called the Impact Scale*. This gives you five clear options. I have found it very useful when negotiating the aim and, if more than one aim, setting time scales for each stage.

1 Eliminate the problem
2 Reduce the problem by degrees
3 Reduce the seriousness of the problem
4 Deal with the problem more efficiently
5 Persuade another to take the lead

*The Impact Scale is based on an idea by Prof John Eck and is used here with his kind permission. Source: John Eck and William Spelman (1987) Problem-Solving: Problem Oriented Policing in Newport News. Washington DC: Police Executive Research Forum.

1. Eliminate the problem

Though this seems to be a popular aim, when set for others, it is really hard to completely eliminate a problem.

There will be occasions when this is an appropriate aim, such as when the Fire Department are called to a house fire. You are hardly going to be happy with an 80% reduction and a leaflet on smoke detectors. Instead, you would like all the flames to be put out and therefore the problem to be eliminated.

To build on the concept of finding those who share your problem, here is a story from World War 2. They had a problem of parachutes not being packed correctly, causing the death of the user. Those who shared the problem were the paratroopers, the aircrews and the senior officers who needed to meet their objective. The story goes that a new manager arrived at the factory packing the parachutes and announced that the parachute packers would be obliged to jump out of an aircraft with one of the parachutes. To ensure that people monitored the work of the others, they would be given one from the store, and not their own. Apparently, the improvement resulted in 100% perfectly packed parachutes.

2. Reduce the problem by degrees

This is most likely to be a numerical target set by yourself or others.
For example, the aim could be to reduce the number of faulty goods coming off a production line to zero by a certain date. Another example is when Local Governments are set a target to reduce the amount of waste going to landfill sites.

3. Reduce the seriousness of the problem

This is the situation where you cannot eliminate or even reduce the problem. In this situation you may just have to focus your efforts and resources on reducing the seriousness of the problem.

For example, let's look at the problem faced by motorists when they are involved in collisions. Over time, cars and coaches have been fitted with seat belts to limit the driver and passengers from hitting parts of the car and each other. Also, to reduce the seriousness of the collisions still further, cars are being fitted with airbags. In this way, although collisions have not been eliminated or even reduced, seat belts and airbags have reduced the seriousness of the injuries to passengers involved in a collision.

4. Deal with the problem more efficiently

When you are at this point you are probably facing the reality that things are really out of control or you have no means to deal with the cause of the problem. Then all your interventions are aimed at managing the consequences and being more efficient at dealing with them.

For example, it could be miners trapped in a tunnel. The fact they are trapped is most likely the result of a collapse within the roof or walls. This was a consequence of mining activity, the existing measures in place to prevent the collapse or the way the rock had been formed.

To be more efficient at dealing with the collapses, the mining industry has set up escape rooms with food and drink at different points within the mines for the miners to seek shelter until they are rescued. This means that, although that part of the tunnel collapsed and the miners were trapped as a consequence, they did not die because they had enough water, food and medical supplies to sustain them until they were rescued. It was such a room as this that enabled the miners trapped in a Chilean mine in 2010 to survive after it took such a long time to rescue them.

5. Persuade another to take the lead

This is the option when you have identified that you, your team or your organisation should not be leading on the problem and that another person, team or organisation should take the lead.

All you need to do is to find the people who have the responsibility and give it to them. They in turn are appreciative and make it clear that any further complaints relating to their problem should go straight to them. Then you wake up and find you have been dreaming!

Getting people to take responsibility for a problem is nearly always going to be a problem in itself. Maybe it is something to do with not wanting to be associated with failure.

I suggest you look at ways described earlier about getting others to share your problem and see if these can be adapted. Probably some form of partnership or coalition is most likely to be the only way to progress things.

Summary

We have defined your Problem, found your Partners and set an Aim. We now need to know far more about the problem, where the demand is coming from and make sense of what is found. The next chapter explains how to go about doing the Research and Analysis.

Who shares your problem?

Chapter 3

Research and Analysis

The purpose of this chapter is to help you:

Find out who wants to have something changed and why

Research and analyse your problem

Partnership Problem Solving Process	
P	Problem and Partner Identification
A	Aim Setting
R	**Research and Analysis**
T	Thinking Creatively
N	Negotiating the Changes
E	Evaluation
R	Recognition and Reward
S	Sharing 'Good Practice'

Chapter 3

Research and Analysis

Introduction

You now need to know as much as you can about the problem, the history, what is happening now and what is likely to be causing it.

What is Research?

Systematic inquiries into a subject in order to discover or revise facts, theories and applications, presented in a detailed, accurate manner.

The reluctance to spend time on the research

An all too common feature of Problem Solving is the situation when people presented with a problem feel compelled to solve it without taking time to really study the problem. I don't know why, but I meet it all the time. Maybe it's their natural make up that prompts them to reach for an immediate solution. Maybe it's conditioning from their work environment. Think about how many recruitment processes include giving the candidate a problem to solve within a set time period. I doubt many people would have progressed through to the next round if they had responded with answers like "before I start on this, could I check to see who wants this resolved and ask them why we should bother?"

I could take this point further and consider how many people would have been selected for the position if they had responded with the statement, "I am concerned that I could make the situation worse, as I don't know enough about this problem, and therefore at this stage I will do nothing". Yet, think about how many problems you have seen that have been made worse by someone making decisions before knowing the facts and the true context of the problems within them.

So, when you are looking at a problem, watch to make sure that you, or the group, do not push on without really getting to know everything about the problem. It is not a popular position to hold, but you have to ask the others, "Are we happy we know enough about the problem before we start committing time and resources to it?"

Identify where the demand to do something is coming from

As well as finding out all about the problem, such as when, where and how long it's been going on, you need to know very early on, what is behind the drive to have something done. In fact, I would recommend that defining the problem, considering an aim and identifying the demand is done almost simultaneously. The three key questions you need to ask to establish the demand are:

1 Who is asking?
2 What is it they want?
3 Why is it important to them?

When asking about the demand you may have to trace back, almost like a family history, to the source of the demand. Sometimes it might be easy, but on other occasions it may have come from a Company Directive, a broader initiative or from legislation. I regularly speak to people tasked with a problem to solve or an action to deliver and they do not know from where it has come and why it is important. If anything, you could at least make a judgement on how much time you devote to it, especially when you are under pressure with a heavy workload.

This approach, though I have discussed it in the world of Problem Solving, is just good practice. For example, at a Military College they make a point in their Leadership course that, as a leader, they should be aware of the military objectives two ranks up, in case circumstances change for themselves, which is inevitable in battle. They can then adapt their actions to meet the overarching objective.

Managing expectations of those making the demand

Another reason to establish early what they want is that they may want something which is unrealistic. It is best, therefore, they know before you embark on the problem solving initiative. It is only when you embark on Problem Solving that you see how unrealistic some expectations are.

For example, people who buy a house facing a park and then complain about children making a noise, or people who buy near a sports ground and then complain about parking problems on a match day. Therefore, before you embark on trying to solve a problem do make sure that the expectations are realistic.

Finding out why?

Another reason why it is important to confirm what it is that someone wants is that you may work towards a solution that misses the point of why they raised the problem in the first place. Therefore, you need to find out what's motivating them to ask for something to be changed. If you don't, you may either miss the point or even make the problem worse.

For example, a Police department in an American city held a public meeting with residents of one of their local government housing projects, in order to find out about the local problems.

They found out that the main problem was the sex workers (previously described as prostitutes) working within their public spaces. The police, to their credit, knew who was raising the problem and what it was, but not why the problem was so important to the residents.

They conscientiously embarked on a police operation based on the assumption that the residents were bothered about their own women being approached by men looking for sex and also the subsequent debris caused by the sexual acts. The chosen tactic was a very heavy presence with their squad cars which resulted in the sex workers being challenged and the men visiting in the cars being stopped.

What the police had not taken the time to find out was why it was a problem to the tenants. The actual problem was the noise. The sex workers worked in the late evening and into the early hours of the morning. The sex workers would fight each other, their clients and their pimps, all of which was creating lots of noise.

The police tactics involved officers challenging the sex workers which resulted in women shouting at the police officers. Arrests would also be taking place with police radios blaring out all the time. Even the stopping of the men in their cars visiting the area meant the use of the vehicles' sirens to alert the drivers. All these incidents were very noisy.

If time had been taken to research specifically who was complaining about the noise, they would have known it was the mothers. Another look at why the noise was a problem would have found that the noise was keeping the children awake when they should have been asleep. As a result, the children were tired at school and subsequently did not do so well in the lessons.

This in turn meant that they would not be achieving their full potential. The mothers wanted their children to achieve good exam results so that they would progress through the education system and be able to leave the area.

Now you know that the noise is "why" it is a problem, you may start thinking of solutions. If we focus on the residents and the noise, you may think about where else do residents have a problem of noise and what is done to placate them. Airports, when they want to increase the number of runways, flights or extend the times they operate, provide the residents, schools etc, with double and triple glazing to negate the effects of the planes' noise. Therefore, could the money spent on policing and prosecuting the offenders be spent instead on fitting double glazing in the homes. I can imagine that if this idea was to be explored, arguments against using local tax dollars would be made.

But we can actually take this further. As the city gets very hot, then the residents would need to open the windows to allow in the fresh cool air, only to negate the point of the double glazing. Then the next step would be to provide air conditioning. If you thought the idea of providing double glazing was not a favoured solution, then the fitting of air conditioning as well would be unlikely to be welcomed. I am not making a judgement on this example, just trying to show you that there are other ways to resolve an issue if you focus on the elements of the problem.

For your information, they neither fitted the double glazing or air conditioner units. They do, however, continue to mount operations and make use of the courts.

Speaking to the people making the demand

When I visit the people who are making the demand I am trying to get an idea of the problem, its context and the severity of it, to see why it is so important to them. What I have seen on many occasions, which is why I am mentioning it in this book, is that there are people who talk-up a problem, in terms of the scale and frequency of the impact it has on themselves and others.

Reasons why people exaggerate the problem

Action	To get something done
	To get it dealt with before other problems
Resources	To get funding
	To keep what funding they have
Personal reasons	To get attention
	To increase their own feeling of importance
	To maintain their position within the group
	To get evidence to support their promotion, own development or election

Please go and visit the problem

I have been in far too many situations when the problems are plotted on a map, or stages of a process written out on flip chart paper and people gather around, stare at it, and then make an assessment on what the problem is. This is okay as a way to get people involved, but not when actions are decided as a result. When I have been in those situations, it reminds me of those magic eye posters in the 1990s where, if you just stared long enough, a 3D picture would emerge from what initially appeared to be random coloured dots. Unfortunately, the same does not happen that, when you stare at the maps a solution emerges.

I cannot stress enough how important it is to go and have a look at the problem, even though it may change when you look at it. The benefits are that you can see the dynamics of the problem and its relationship with everything around it. The visit will also enable you to see the problem in context, other influences and other people who also share the problem, your potential partners.

For example, I visited a large retail park in West London, near to the River Thames. They had found a dead body lying in a car park, consistent with a fall. The person had literally appeared from nowhere. It was not the only body that had been found in similar circumstances.

You could speculate that they had ended up in this area having fallen from a building, though none were near, or fallen from a vehicle, though the area was secure. (It is not the urban myth of the scuba diver, sucked up with the water from a lake to douse the nearby forest fire).

However, being present at the location you know within minutes the reason for the bodies. This is because this area is on the flight path to Heathrow airport and, as the planes turn south following the river, this is the point where pilots lower the undercarriage. Stowaways, having climbed into the wheel section prior to taking off, would die as a result of the freezing temperatures' during the flight. They would then fall to earth as the wheels were lowered. This is why the bodies were found nowhere near to anything else. The most recent example was in September 2012 in Mortlake, South West London.

When you undertake the site visit try and find someone who can guide you, as they can show you the nuances of the problem, the significance of any events taking place and evidence that something has happened. For example, when examining for the presence of infestation of woodworm, an experienced person in that area will look for the signs that others would miss.

Please take your time. Stand still and take everything in. It's a bit like looking into a river. Initially, you will only see the water but, after a short period of time, you will see items on the riverbed, the flow of the river and the fish. You need to see all the elements that make up your problem.

I also recommend that you take a camera to capture the problem, the scale and its position to other points of interest. These pictures are also very useful when you need to illustrate a report or a presentation.

Get the history

It may be that something was done to resolve a problem, and even held up as a great example for the company, but which inadvertently caused another problem. This is risky as a Problem Solver, as you may start investigating something that had been seen as a great success. Some people are not going to welcome the fact that you are, not only doubting whether it was as good as it was said to be, but considering it to be the cause of the current problem. The crux will come when you define the problem.

By looking at history, you will also get an idea of how long it has been a problem. If it has been a problem for decades, then this must have influence on the time scale when setting the aim.

Problems can change when you look at them

You could be inspecting processes within an organisation and the presence of someone from 'Head Office' results in everything being done by the book, and all those short cuts that cause the problems are set aside until the visit is over. This has led to expressions adapted from "what gets measured gets done" to "what gets measured gets altered."

As a result, sometimes those needing to see the reality of a situation go undercover to identify the real problems and the methods employed to resolve them or mask them. This is why TV programmes that feature bosses going back to the ground floor are so informative for those taking part and why companies employ mystery customers. However, one fast food chain insists that the mystery customer asks for a receipt. This seems to negate the very point of being unknown to the staff, as so few customers ask for a receipt. We could be cynical here and think that the person insisting on this procedure does not want any problems to be found.

Talk to other people who are there

When you start to look at the problem, don't limit your contact to those making the demand. Members of staff that have been there for years or recently retired and those who have left the organisation are a great source of information and likely to be more open about the situation. Sometimes, however, they are very negative and sometimes "they always come out well, when retelling the story."

Discrepancies of the problem, or its scale

Earlier we looked at how the problem is sometimes talked up by those making the demand. When I start researching the problem, I sometimes encounter the opposite situation, where people talk down the problem. Here are some of the reasons that I believe account for this discrepancy.

They are responsible for it.

They did something that made the problem worse.

They feel they should have done more themselves earlier and do not want to admit that fact.

They do not want the attention on themselves or their team.

They are going for promotion or another job.

They want to delay any actions, as they are not ready for the solution.

They benefit from it being around.
For example, I have seen maintenance crews benefit from the overtime paid out to deal with a recurring problem.

They want another problem dealt with instead.

They don't like the person making the demand.

This last point is fairly common, normally brought about because the people tasked with resolving the problem have been alienated. It is very hard for them to look at a problem when the person making the demand feels the need to involve everyone, including senior personnel and the media, and who unfairly describes their failings when they have been doing their best in the task.

Think about the person being interviewed

Too often in an interview people are not listening but instead are just waiting for the other person to finish so they can either say what they want to say or ask their next question. As well as thinking about your questions, you need to keep in mind the person you are talking to and ask a follow up question from the information just given.

Some people can become uncomfortable with your presence so explain the purpose of the talk as soon as possible, especially if you are from head office or have been brought in from outside. There may be other things going on, and they may connect your visit to these other events.

Check to see how much time they have for the interview. Tell them how much time you have and, if more time is going to be needed, then arrange a date and time before the interview starts. Explain that you may need to make notes and that they can see what you are writing at any time.

Have consideration for the person being asked a number of questions. They may feel threatened or embarrassed, especially if they do not know the answer to some of your questions. The person being interviewed may also be suspicious of the interview. How do you know that they had not been treated well previously, or that they know of someone who had got into trouble because they were interviewed?

The opening from you should explain who you are, the purpose of the interview and a summary of the situation / problem you want to talk about. The first interview question could be "please tell me about it" or something equally broad. Then let them speak. Take notes if you have a question for later. They will be getting a measure of you and how you respond. This is when you need to encourage them with nods, smiles and the occasional summary. Expect them to go on.

You need to encourage the person with reassuring terms, such as "okay, please keep going" and allow them to repeat themselves. You need to allow them to go off the point and in depth, as this is when clues to the problem emerge. The term is 'narrative rich' and is very useful as you find the nuances of a problem and information that may not have surfaced with your structured questions. Offer that they can make use of sketches and can refer to any notes they may have made.

Later, thank them by a letter, phone call or email. You could even send them a copy of your research and analysis and see if they agree. Over time they may have thought of something else or seen something else and this gives them an opportunity to pass it on to you. They may be someone you could ask about the problem when you are at the Evaluation stage.

Good questions to ask about the problem

Asking good questions will help you in getting to know all about the problem and is called Convergent Research. Here are the ones used most.

What's going on?

What is the problem?

Is the problem getting bigger, smaller or staying the same?

What is distinctive about it?

What is the same when the problem occurs?

What is different when the problem occurs?

What is causing the problem?

What are the consequences of the problem?

What happened when it became worse and immediately before?

Who is involved?

Who is causing the problem?

Who is affected by the problem?

Who else is working on the problem?

When?

When did the problem occur?

When is it worse?

How?

How long has it been a problem?

How much is the problem costing?

Where?

Where is the problem?

Where does it happen the most?

Ways you can ask your questions

When talking to someone, just asking questions starting with "who, what and where" can be rather unsettling and not always focused enough on the problem. Instead, you could use a method called TED PIE. You select your topic and which area you want to know more about. You then select a first set of prompts, put it with another set and then the rest of the question. For example, "Describe, exactly how the rats are getting into the house?"

Tell me		Explain		Describe	
Precisely		In detail		Exactly	
Who	What	Where	When	How	Why
Followed by your question					

Opposites

So far the questions have been all about the problem. There is a different approach to asking questions and it is to ask the 'opposites'. It is the approach to use when you are trying to make comparisons.

Here are some 'opposite' type questions.

Who?

Who is not causing the problem?

Who is not affected by the problem?

When?

When is the problem not present?

What?

What is different when the problem does not occur?

What happened when it became better?

Where?

Where is there no problem?

In effect the cold spots of a map. Normally when looking at a hotspot, the dots are in red and you get drawn to that part of the map or process. Take time to look at the other areas and ask why.

Others

Who does not share your problem?

Who is benefiting from the problem?

It does take time to get used to using them. When you get comfortable, you should mix them in with your regular questions. It is a very effective way of getting more information and on occasions can actually generate solutions. We will return to the 'opposites' when we are thinking about generating ideas to solve the problem.

Where are you now with the problem?

Baseline

A baseline is a measure of the problem, in effect where you are right now. This in turn will make it easier to show you whether the actions employed are having any effect on the problem. Otherwise you would never know if what you were doing was working or actually making the problem worse. Finally, it will help you to determine whether you achieved your aim.

For example, if you decided to go on a diet, you would need to measure things like your body weight, your body mass index or your waist size to give you a measure of where you are at the start of the diet and whether the changes you make are having some impact.

Creating your own database

You could start counting things already taking place. If the problem is that you have too many people waiting in the queue at your store, then you could count the numbers in the queue. You could capture the baseline by taking photographs. You could, instead, use other measures, such as the time taken to get served or the existing customer satisfaction rating.

Spread your bets

You could use a number of different sources for your baseline. A wide range of indicators all showing the same thing will give your work and success more credibility. You should use the same methods at the end of your project when you are evaluating it.

I use the term direct and indirect measures when assessing the methods used. Direct measures are things you could measure that are most closely related to your problem. For example, if a High Street was concerned about the decline in business, direct measures would be the number of customers visiting the area, known as 'foot fall', or best of all, the amount of money spent. However, information on the customers visiting and spending in a store is going to be of value to competitors, which means that a store may not be happy to hand over such valuable data.

An indirect measure would be the number of cars in the car park, but they may be parking there for other reasons, such as a local event or to use the train. Another indirect measure would be the amount of litter swept from the streets. There already exists a litter index, and the amount of rubbish being collected could give you an idea of the numbers of people coming. Again, they might not be buying as much and some fast food stores collect their own, but if you use a number of indicators the more chances you will get of seeing how many people are coming to the area.

The Analysis - making sense of the Research

When you have undertaken your research, you are going to have to undertake some analysis, which is making sense of what you have found. In short, the reason **why?**

For example, if you find that part of an internal facing wall of your house is wet, you only know at this point that you have a wet wall. You could touch it with a towel which, if it became soaked, would show that the wall is very wet. If you find mould you would know it has been wet for a while but you would not know why the wall was wet. Further research would include looking outside, to see what is happening, such as a broken pipe.

Finding nothing, you would have to return to your wall and remove the plaster and brick work, in effect deeper research, to find out more. If you find a water pipe you would check to see if it is leaking. It is leaking, so now you know the problem is a leaking pipe and that the wet wall is just the consequence. All the time you were trying to make sense of what you had found.

Analytical Techniques

There are many ways to make sense of your research and these are described as analytical techniques. Here are my two favourite ones.

Why? Why? Why? Analysis

Firstly, summarise the problem. Then ask the question "Why might the problem exist?" (Use might at this stage as we may not know the definite reasons, only the possible reasons). Then ask 'Why?' again against each of the reasons given, normally between 3 and 5 times to get the answer. If you have children they can easily pass 5 "why's?". The answer from the parent normally ends in "because I told you so."

Pareto or the 80 / 20 Principle

This is the principle that a universal five to one ratio exists, which can be helpful to use when analysing your research findings. For example, if you are a manager, then 20% of your staff cause you 80% of your problems. Also that 20% of your customers make 80% of your profits. There have been many studies that support such a principle and the benefit for you is that it can help you focus your efforts into one distinct area, when you do not have access to an analyst. I see it most often when I return from holiday and there is a build up of emails. I find it only takes 20% effort to clear 80% of them, but 80% effort to clear the last 20%. By the way, this method only works 80% of the time!

Inference

When you do not know enough about a problem, even after your research, you may have to infer what it is? Inference is "The act of reasoning from factual knowledge or evidence."

A way to do this is to make a tentative hypothesis in order to explain the facts and observations. The less you know the more you need to infer the cause.

For example, in Victorian London there was a cholera epidemic. The cause was unknown. The research could tell you that people died from cholera; who had died; where they had died and when, but not what was causing it, the "why?" One belief was that it was "bad air". This changed due to the work of a Dr John Snow. He formed his hypothesis, which was that cholera was a waterborne disease. He had no way to prove his theory so he mapped the deaths and interviewed the locals. This identified that the source of the water drunk by those infected was a water pump in Broad Street. He examined the water but his findings were not conclusive.

So he had the pump's handle removed which prevented people from drawing drinking water from that specific water supply, which was not an easy thing to do. This in turn resulted in no more people becoming infected in that immediate area. He had proved his hypothesis to be correct and that it was the water drawn by the pump that carried the disease. This in turn confirmed that cholera was a waterborne disease.

However, an inference could be wrong.

Here is an example where the inference is open to debate, and more research will be required. In 2011, a study was undertaken by Pearson the publishers. Teachers were asked to identify points where boys would switch off in class when novels were being read. Nearly a third of the teachers questioned said boys were put off before the book had even been opened if they saw it had more than 200 pages. You could infer that this is why girls read more than boys.

However, you could look at the books the boys were being asked to read. Are the books being offered, described as the 'classics', books they are obliged to read, as opposed to ones they want to read? It may have nothing to do with the length of the book. Maybe the study should include offering the boys books from the Harry Potter series or Lord of the Rings, then see what they do. These are read avidly by boys and they are far longer than 200 pages.

Redefining your problem and resetting your aim

As we are working methodically through each stage of a Problem Solving Process to ensure each point is covered we will, by the very nature of the process, be looking and thinking about different stages. For example, as soon as you are looking at a problem, you will be thinking about solutions. There is a risk, however, that you research these ideas instead of researching the problem. Also, you may start putting in actions only to discover that you actually have two problems.

Therefore, we need to use the Problem Solving Stages as a guide and not a one way highway. This will allow you to move easily from one thing to another. To bind yourself to an inflexible structure does not work, as anyone who has dialled a Call Centre will appreciate. There is frustration when there are only limited prompts and your problem does not follow the order they predicted. You then have to try a different route or wait for the operator.

We are at one of those points of the Problem Solving Process where we are likely to have to go back on ourselves. For example, we have just completed the Research and Analysis stage and have made sense of what we have found. As a result, we are most likely to have redefined our Problem and are ready to set an achievable aim.

Here is an example of how the Research and Analysis of a Problem changed the Problem and the Aim.

A few years ago some friends bought a house to renovate and sell on. After improving the house they turned their attention to the problem of the overgrown garden. Growing amongst the common weeds were three bamboo looking plants. They set the aim as 'Eliminating the problem of these weeds'. They removed the tops of the plants, with the intention of killing it, and dug in the rest of the plant. This method had always worked before and they believed their aim was realistic.

However, the 'bamboo' shoots returned, but now there were twice as many as before. They repeated the same process, as this method had always worked before in previous gardens, so they had no reason to change their practice. They just thought they had not been as thorough as they should have been. The Problem and Aim remained the same. However, the number of shoots doubled again and so it was time for some more detailed research.

They already knew where the problem was, how much of a problem it was and when it was problem. They needed to know what it was. Samples were taken to a local garden centre and it did not take long to identify the 'bamboo' as Japanese Knotweed.

If you are unfamiliar with it, look it up on the Internet which is what they did, and it was not comfortable reading. One entry suggested that the gardener "should treat it like a hobby", as it was almost impossible to clear. As a result, the Problem and the Aim had to change. This is also a good example to show how the Impact Scale can be applied to the problem.

The aim initially was to eliminate the problem. However the research showed that with tremendous effort and cost they would just about reduce the problem. Meanwhile, they were being more efficient at treating it by bagging it and then burning it. Another option could have been to reduce the seriousness of the problem and concentrate all their efforts to stop it from spreading towards the house, as it can grow through concrete! Finally, they could let another agency take the lead by selling the house and telling prospective buyers about the problem.

The rest of the example is just to finish off the story. What they did, from the advice given, was to cut it all down, clear as many of the plants as possible and wait for the new shoots to grow. These new shoots were then sprayed with a weed killer.

The dead growth was cleared and the process repeated. It took three years for it to be brought under control.

At the time of writing, there have been two developments. Firstly, a 2mm insect, Aphalara itadori, a type of psyllid, jumping plant lice, that eats Japanese knotweed in its homeland, has been found. The other is the discovery of the Leafspot fungus. This was found to only damage the Japanese Knotweed and is regarded as having the most potential for controlling the plant, though it is not expected to eradicate it.

There are a few lessons from this. The result of research showed that you had to go back to the process and redefine your problem. You also had to reset your aim from 'eliminate in one year' to 'eliminate in 5 years'. You learnt that some tactics need time and you should not expect instant results and give up when they appear to be failing. Finally, look in the garden more closely next time you go house hunting and wait for the spring!

Summary

This chapter has helped you to consider where the demand to do something comes from, given you a range of methods to research the problem and ways to analyse your problem. The next chapter is all about finding ways to resolve your problem and meet your aim.

Who shares your problem?

Chapter 4

Thinking Creatively

The purpose of this chapter is to help you:

Feel confident about taking time to think and to generate options

Be inspired by others, make connections and create your own ideas

Partnership Problem Solving Process	
P	Problem and Partner Identification
A	Aim Setting
R	Research and Analysis
T	**Thinking Creatively**
N	Negotiating the Changes
E	Evaluation
R	Recognition and Reward
S	Sharing 'Good Practice'

Chapter 4

Thinking Creatively

Introduction

Now that you have spent time getting to know all about the problem, you will naturally want to solve it, or at least reduce the impact it is having. This chapter is going to look at 'thinking' which, although obvious, is too often neglected. The benefit of thinking is it allows ideas to form in your mind, which in turn could lead to actions you had not thought about using to tackle the problem. We will then be looking at getting ideas from other areas and the advantages of working with others to generate further ideas or to hone ones already created.

I wish I had thought of that

There are going to be problems that are really difficult to solve. In fact, we looked earlier at using the Impact Scale when deciding at what point we are going to set our aim. Eliminating the problem was not the only solution.

As you work through the different Problem Solving stages you will get to a point where you know what the problem is and you are moving towards developing actions to resolve it. This is when it's a good time to just have a think. I appreciate there is pressure on you to act, but do try and find time to actually consider what you have.

When you need to think, this is best done alone. It maybe that you take yourself away from the problem or the people, or you immerse yourself in the problem, maybe by visiting it again, but this time on your own.

It is the opportunity to think that will enable you to see patterns, make connections, and allow other ideas to surface. So please resist the pressure to do something as much as you can, and have a think.

I personally get distracted by noise, and open plan offices cause me real difficulties. In fact, I worked for a manager who was very task orientated and was very good at his job. However, he was uncomfortable with me just sitting there thinking. He would look over and was only happy when I was typing something. In the end I had to go on visits to other departments but, in truth, I would just sit in different places to think.

Here is a problem for you to think about.

As part of your trip you need to catch the 6.15am ferry. You are alone and have arrived late in the evening. You know that it is going to be a long drive the next day and would welcome the sleep. However, your mobile phone has limited charge and you are not that confident that your phone will have enough charge to last you until the morning. The only shop open now is a small food store and it doesn't sell alarm clocks.

What are your thoughts? Here are my ideas.

Don't sleep

Sleep on the ferry

Sleep when you get off the ferry

Catch a later ferry

Is there another way of crossing the water?

Park across the gates so they have to wake you up in order to get people onto the ferry

Find a security guard nearby and pay them to wake you up.
I think that would be a case of pay half now and half later.

Buy some bread and spread it on your roof. Then, when the birds in the morning see your food, they land on your metal car roof and the noise of pecking at the bread wakes you up.

Those were some ideas, had you thought of any others? The point is that there are normally a number of ways something can be done. Sometimes you can think about it and solve it yourself, sometimes you need some inspiration or sometimes the ideas come from working in a group. I wonder how many more ideas we could have produced if we had been able to spark off ideas from each other. Think about the wonderful songs that are written as a result of the collaboration between two song writers.

Cross fertilization of ideas

So far our research has been focused on the problem of "where, when, how long?" etc. Now it is time to examine the elements of your problem to see how they may have been dealt with elsewhere. For example, if you wanted to prevent road injuries on a public road, go and see the latest developments with Grand Prix racing. They invest heavily in securing the safety of their drivers and the roadside spectators.

Initially, you need to break down your problem into its component parts and, for each part, find out how the same, or similar problems, are tackled in other situations, to see if those solutions could be applied to your problem.

Here is an example of this process.

Imagine you are a Hotel Manager and you have been receiving complaints about your slow lift. After doing your research you have confirmed that your problem can be defined as "Your only lift has congestion between 8 and 9 in the mornings during the conference season".

Your baseline is that there are, on average, 15 people waiting in the lobby for the lift and the lift only holds 5 people. (Another base line could be how long it takes people to get back to their room between 8 and 9 in the morning, compared to average throughout the day).

Your aim is "to reduce the congestion, from 15 to 5 people, between 8am and 9am, in the conference season, by a certain time" (set a date).

If you are at the point of generating ideas, the constituent elements of the problem to be examined are hotels, lifts and congestion.

Stage 1. Other hotels with lift congestion

You would want to interview other hotel owners who have, or have had, a problem of congestion with their lifts. For those who had resolved it, you would want to know what they had done and what they would not do again. You would need to find out from others who still have the problem: what they had tried; what they are currently applying and what they are considering.

You then take all these suggestions and see if they would work for your problem. You have to be careful not to apply a straight copy. Just because it worked for them, may not mean it would work in your circumstances.

Stage 2. Other situations with lift congestion

You would then want to look at other situations where there are lifts and where they have, or have had, congestion.

For example, some shopping centres provide escalators as alternatives. Some places recommend using the stairs and even mention how many calories a person would burn if they did so.

Car parks have lifts that only stop at alternate levels. Some high rise buildings have different lifts for different levels. As before, you need to take those ideas back to your problem to see if they would be suitable.

Stage 3. Other situations with congestion.

You would then look only at the problem of congestion.

For example, banks have queues at certain times and they have people whose role it is to go along the queue and see if they are able to answer a question or use another facility, such as a paying in machine. This is known as 'queue-combing'. At airports, these queue-combers make sure people have their tickets and passports ready.

On some roads, to reduce congestion they charge at certain times. Again, take those ideas back and see if they would be suitable.

For example, would charging people to use the lift be more trouble than it's worth. However, an alternative to this would be to offer a financial reward, such as a discount, if they did not use the lift at certain times. They do that on railways with off peak discounts and health and fitness centres have cheaper packages if the user only visits at certain times, so it has been done successfully elsewhere.

Learning from Nature

Here are some examples of the impressive utilisation of ideas gleaned from Nature's solutions to problems.

The manufacture of plasterboard was inspired by the way wasps use hexagonal shapes to strengthen the walls of the nest. In fact, not only do the wasps create their own wood pulp, the hexagonal shape is the most efficient shape to reduce the number of walls you need to use, which reduces the amount of pulp needed and the weight of the product.

Another example is how the medical profession is learning from sharks to deal with problem of bacteria growing on surfaces. Studies have revealed that the surface of the shark is covered in dermal denticles. These create a surface on which bacteria, or anything else, cannot take hold. This means that surfaces in hospitals can also be coated with the same shapes to prevent bacteria growing.

Another industry which is also benefitting from the knowledge of the sharks skin, is the Shipping and Submarine industry. This is because the same surface prevents barnacles taking hold, and the removal of barnacles from ships is an expensive procedure.

Finally, these same dermal denticles also inspired Speedo in 2000 to produce swimwear called 'Fast skin'. This enables the wearer to move more easily through water. It proved so successful that it has been banned by the Olympic Committee.

Learning from others

Now that you are clear about your problem, you could seek others who have the same problem, and those who had it but who have it no more.

The benefit of finding others who are also working on the same problem is that it is a great way to find partners. However, this would not work if overcoming a problem everyone is facing has commercial implications. For example, finding a way to reduce the glare on the electronic books, would not be something you would like to share with your rival companies.

However, if you had a problem of rat infestation in your property, then there is going to be a good chance that there will be others willing to share with you how they resolved it, especially if it is a neighbour who is going to share your problem if it's not resolved. The advantage of finding people who are also suffering from the same problem is that they will already have experience of different methods to try to resolve it, and even tell you what not to do!

Each of their actions needs to be looked at, as they may have misused an effective method. At the same time, you may be offered advice which comes from someone who happens to be selling the product. You have to be careful as they may not be unbiased.

Learning from history

There are so many problems that have been overcome in the past which can provide you with ideas to resolve your current problem. For example, when NASA was designing the astronaut's suit, they had to balance the competing demands of the user, one that protects the wearer but is also flexible. This same problem was faced by medieval knights. As a result, the armour used for Henry VIII was examined and its construction and overlapping pieces inspired the designers of the Apollo space suits.

There are companies who spend time and money collecting information for commercial purposes, such as an up to date electronic mailing list, only to find it is then copied by others, who have not paid for it. For those employed in this industry this is a real problem and they have learnt from others who have faced the same problem. For example, map makers have for centuries had the problem of people copying their maps. They had spent time and money going to these places and then producing the map. It would not take long for someone to copy it and pass it off as work they had done themselves. So, all map makers add things onto the map that do not exist. It could be a small road, a stream or even a village.

It is easy for them to check another's map and see if the fictitious place is mentioned. So, for those who compile mailing lists they add a fictional company title together with their own address. When they then receive a mail shot addressed to the fictional company at their own address, from a company who has not paid for their list, they contact the company and inform them that they have breached copyright and that recompense is required. It is a very successful method.

Other useful sources of information

Go onto the internet and just follow different links and see what you can find.

Go onto the internet and seek out specialist websites.

Visit discussion forums and ask your question.

Read the trade magazines.

Seek out research documents on the subject.

Find out if there is a trade association or interest group.

Go to Amazon and find the relevant 'How to...' book.

Creativity

Once you have had an opportunity to think about the problem and seen how others have done things, the next stage is to generate ideas.

Types of Creativity – Radical and Incremental

Creativity can be either a combination of existing ideas in a new format, or thinking of something new. The approach I use is to separate creativity into Radical and Incremental Creativity. Radical Creativity is doing something new, while Incremental Creativity is making smaller changes.

For example, the first machine to clean houses was the carpet sweeper. Its arrival, having been the first on the market, would have been a radical change. Over time, there were incremental changes to improve the machines. The next radical change was the arrival of the electrical vacuum cleaner, which again was improved incrementally over time. Then the next radical change was the Dyson cyclone vacuum cleaner. Since its arrival there have been a number of incremental improvements to the product, but the radical principle has remained the same.

The Dyson cleaner is another example of the cross fertilization of ideas. Apparently, Mr Dyson, the inventor of the Dyson cyclone vacuum cleaner, was at a sawmill when he noticed that sawdust was being removed from the building by the use of large industrial cyclones, which were sucking out the dust. He used the same principle for his cleaners. (The Journal of Business and Design vol. 8, no. 1).

Creating ideas with one other person

When generating ideas, you may find it more productive to generate ideas with one other person. I have someone with who I have a really creative rapport. When we are working together, we almost climb over each other to get our thoughts and ideas out. One of the reasons it works so well, is that we can voice our thoughts aloud, without fear of criticism.

I have run creative sessions with young people using the same scenarios as used with adults. Their ideas are no different from the adults, but the noticeable difference is that they are busy pushing forward their own ideas rather than criticising the ideas of the others.

Creating ideas in a group

Generating ideas in groups can be electrifying, with people charged with a type of static energy as they share ideas, only to have others take hold of their ideas and develop them further, described as 'piggy backing'.

How to create an environment for the group to succeed

Just as there are benefits of thinking alone, so working with others to create ideas and make connections is of equal value. For example, it allows someone else to take an idea and refine it immediately. The term 'piggy backing' is when someone develops the ideas of others. It is so exhilarating, especially when the ideas are forming faster than they can be expressed. Sometimes in the rush to give out their ideas, they are misunderstood by others and even this very misunderstanding takes the line of thought into a different direction and even more ideas are created.

What information should be given out?

Prior to the session you could send out the problem, the aim and any research, as this enables people to consider the problem before the main event.

Where to hold the meeting?

Use a room big enough to allow for heated discussions and space to spread out. Also enough space for flip chart stands and wipe boards.

You could allow the meeting to be at the site of the problem. This has advantages such as putting the ideas into context and being inspired by the surroundings. However, the venue may be noisy and not conducive to creative thought. It could also have problems with accessibility or even be dangerous to those attending.

When to hold it?

Arrange a time that is suitable for people, even if you have to run a number of sessions to cover the times. Avoid having it at the end of a working day because some people may need to get home and therefore will not be keen to think of anything that could delay them.

How long to run the session?

I would suggest about 2 hours. But be strict on the time and make it clear when the session is going to end. If you overrun and make it awkward for people to leave, you run the risk that they will not come again.

So, how do we generate ideas?

Make the problem a question.

To generate ideas, phrase the problem as a question.

For example it could start with "How can we...? Further still, you could make it positive such as "How can we get more....?

Fashion retailers could ask "How can we reduce 'grab and run' thefts?" Clothes shops have a problem of thieves grabbing handfuls of clothes off a rack and running out of the store. Not the most sophisticated method, compared to the lengths some thieves go to overcome the electronic tagging, but still effective. One way to prevent this method is for the shop staff to still hang up the clothes on the rail, but make sure that every other one is hung up the opposite way. In that way, when the thief grabs the clothes, he or she cannot pull them off the rail and flee the shop.

You could then employ one of the idea generating techniques available. There are many tools and techniques used to analyse your problem, and the same goes for techniques to generate ideas.

There are so many that, for me to list each one and explain it with an example, it would need another book. Instead, I recommend a book called "101 Creative Problem Solving Techniques" by James M Higgins. In my opinion, it is the best book available on that topic.

Look at that problem, but from another area.

Here is an example of learning from another situation. To get fibre optic cables through existing underground pipes, has the problem of getting them through the existing labyrinth of tunnels. One very costly and time consuming method is for the companies to dig up the pipes and relay them, together with their own pipe work.

Instead they employ ferrets. They attach a string to a ferret. The string is then tied to the cable and the animal dropped into the tunnel and encouraged to make its way through the maze of tiny and twisted pipes to a desired point. Just as people use ferrets to hunt rabbits, by dropping the ferrets into the complex tunnels.

Another variation of the use of 'opposites'

We previously used the 'opposite' questions when undertaking the research. It is also a very effective way to generate solutions.

Here is an example of 'opposites' from the airline industry.

Those employed to load freight onto the aircraft had a problem of moving the large purpose built containers through the warehouse and into the cargo section of aircraft. The normal solution is to put the containers on wheels, which would work well with moving these huge containers around the warehouse, but not very good when inside the aircraft, as they are likely to move around during the flight. Yet, wheels or rollers would be ideal. The problem was resolved using an 'opposite' technique. Instead of the wheels being fitted onto the container, they integrated small wheels across the entire floor of the warehouse. In that way the containers could be moved easily and then finally pushed onto the aircraft.

Finally, I facilitated a Problem Solving session on the problem of drive-by shootings. Instead of asking the group the usual opener of 'How can we stop drive-by shootings?', I asked the group "How could we increase their success?" This time more ideas came forward that had not previously been thought about. This led to the question "What does a marksman need to be successful?" The answer was that they need a steady base, such as a tripod. In the light of this requirement, I suggested putting in rumble strips along the stretch of road where most shootings were taking place. (Rumble strips are designed to slow down motorists.) In that way, the car would shudder and it would prove too difficult to take aim and maybe the machine gun would also jam.

Innovation

Innovation is the practical application of the idea. It is the part of the problem solving session where you have to be ruthless with the ideas. This can be difficult if it sounds good and everyone is very enthusiastic. But, and it is a really big but, unless an idea can be successfully applied, then it will fail. In the TV Programme 'Dragons Den', at some point the inventor will be asked some 'make or break' questions, such as, "what is this product trying to solve?" and "what does your project do to meet that need?" and "how easy is it to use?"

Therefore, after you have developed your ideas, you need to ask people what they think, and really focus on what could prevent having the idea successfully applied. Then ask them how they would resolve that point. You could then make your own suggestion and again ask them what would stop it working and what could go wrong if it was put in place.

Maybe you need to find those people who are always negative. I think you know the ones I mean. They are the type of people "where every silver lining has a cloud". Find them, and ask them what they think. The more you test your ideas at this time the better.

Sustainability

One factor you need to consider is the sustainability of any of your ideas.

For example, a town in Scotland had a problem with the use of their public football pitches. There were two full sized pitches, divided by a busy road. Those aged between 10 and 14 would only be allowed by their parents to play on the pitch nearest their homes.

Later in the day, they would be forced off this pitch by the teenagers who were also not allowed by their parents to cross the road and play on the other pitch. In turn, the young men of the town would push the teenagers off the pitch.

They could have introduced rules about who could use the pitches at certain times. As this would have to be done on a regular basis, I am sure it would have resulted in a number of confrontations between those employed to enforce the rules and those playing football. Fortunately, a more sustainable solution was implemented.

To prevent young men dominating football pitches, the Park Manager divided the nearest pitch into one third and two thirds. The young ones played on the 1/3 size, the teenagers played on the 2/3 pitch and the young men, had no choice but to cross the road to play on the full sized pitch.

Other ideas, once implemented, may need a system or funding to keep them working, such as maintenance. For example, you may have introduced a signage to move people more efficiently around an airport. However, the signage may fade, break off or even be blocked at a later date. You would therefore have to employ people to regularly check the condition of the signage and check that nothing had been placed in front of it. Therefore, when coming up with your ideas, you may have to create other ideas to ensure its sustainability. You could offer a reward to someone who had difficulty reading your sign and had taken the time to report it. The reward could work out cheaper and they may in turn add a suggestion to resolve it. You could even make it a game for children to play when they are at the airport.

Summary

This chapter looked at how we need to think about a problem and how it could be resolved. We examined how elements of the problem may have been dealt with by others in other situations and how this information could give inspiration to our thought processes. We looked at the creative thinking process and explored different ways to generate ideas.

The next chapter helps us to put those ideas into action.

Who shares your problem?

Chapter 5

Negotiating the Changes

The purpose of this chapter is to help you:

Negotiate agreement to the Action Plan

Monitor the action

Undertake a risk assessment

Partnership Problem Solving Process	
P	Problem and Partner Identification
A	Aim Setting
R	Research and Analysis
T	Thinking Creatively
N	**Negotiating the Changes**
E	Evaluation
R	Recognition and Reward
S	Sharing 'Good Practice'

Chapter 5

Negotiating the Changes

Introduction

There will be a point when it's time to start making changes. It is not going to be easy. This chapter helps you plan your actions, suggests ways you can get the agreement of others and how to manage events to reduce the chances of things going wrong.

Your action plan

Putting actions in place can be very testing. This is where a number of initiatives go no further, or the responses end up as merely pointless activities with very little impact on the problem. To make a difference you will have to be able to coordinate a series of actions, similar to a musical conductor.

It maybe that one action is needed to be done by another or the same action needs to be done by a number of different people. It maybe that one person or organisation has to do a number of actions or a different action needs to be completed by different people. Just to make it even harder, some of these actions will need to be done simultaneously, while others will need to be done sequentially to be effective. This is even more testing if it is being done across a partnership.

For example, in some places school children at the end of the day all use the same bus stop to go home. Rivalries exist and unfortunately fights sometimes take place as a result. This problem has been resolved by schools staggering the times they end the school day and by the bus companies ensuring that there are enough buses to pick up the children at the critical times. These actions not only had to be coordinated but negotiation and sales skills were needed by those tasked to resolve the problem with the local bus company, schools and parents.

Finding your own champion

If you are working on a problem and you need support, it does not have to be just financial but could be a change in policy, it is going to be useful to have someone to supply this support for you.

These people are normally higher up the organisation, where the demand was from in the first place before it was directed downwards for something to be done. If you are having difficulty in implementing their wishes, for the lack of funding or anything else, then they can be approached for support. My advice is not to make too many requests to this person, but to seek their ideas as well as offering your solution.

Getting agreement with others

It is crucial to get the cooperation of others. My approach is to focus my efforts on those who can enable the changes to take place. These people are described as being "the junctions of influence". They are not necessarily the heads of departments but have the ability to influence what does, and what does not, get done.

You will find them in all industries, sometimes they are the ones who have been there the longest, hold a supervisory role or have the strength of character to move others to what they want to happen. You may yourself be that person who is the junction of influence. My advice is to find the right people to get on your side. It is not always easy, as some will work on 'not showing out'.

However, don't make the mistake of thinking that just because they are not visible they do not have the expertise, motivation and capacity to manipulate events. I have found the best way is to negotiate with these people, especially as they are going to be very knowledgeable and can be your greatest allies.

Selling is an important skill in Problem Solving. It will help you sell to others the idea of working in partnership with you, the reasons for supporting your actions and the fact that effective Problem Solving can sometimes take time. Don't try to sell the entire approach at the first meeting. Allow time for the other person to think and reflect. Sometimes you may only sell another meeting. Prepare alternatives. If you can't make your primary objective, have a fallback position ready.

Trade off

A very effective form of negotiation with other organisations is the 'Trade-off'. This works rather like bartering. Firstly, look for something that is expensive for them but cheap for you 'expensive' and 'cheap' doesn't just refer to finance, it can also mean staff hours, resources etc. Next, look for something that is cheap for them but expensive for you. Then **Swap.**

For example in the 1870's relationships were developing between Japan and the United Kingdom. Both had expertise in specific areas but wanted to become proficient in other areas and so they decided to swap what they were good at. The Japanese provided art and fabric samples and, in return, the City of Glasgow provided knowledge on engineering.

Questions to be asked as you put your plan together

People   Who will our ideas affect?

How might we gain their acceptance?

How might we best gain support for our idea?

How might we best present our proposal?

Partners   What positive impact would this have on our partners?

What negative impact would this have on our partners?

How will we keep our partners informed of our progress?

Application   Can the actions be sustained?

What resources are needed to implement our idea?

What might go wrong and why?

What can we do to prevent these problems?

If we cannot prevent them, how might we overcome these problems?

Monitoring   At what point will the actions be monitored?

Who would do it?

What would they need from us?

Setting an Action Plan

Here are points to consider when you produce your Action Plan.

Part 1 – What you want done

Describe the actions required and state them as an Objective. This needs to be SMART with consideration to the Impact Scale as discussed in earlier chapters.

What processes or policies need to be changed for the actions to be progressed?

How much latitude is going to be given to make any changes to the way it's done?

Part 2 – What people are needed

Who is going to take the lead for the response? Who is going to be the deputy?

How specific do you want to be. This is going to be a balance between giving people flexibility and making sure it's done correctly. Would a diagram, map or template help?

Do people need extra information or extra skills, such as additional training?

How much money, facilities and transport are needed for the actions to take place or for those doing the actions?

Part 3 – When you want it done

When will it start?

How much time is going to be given to each task?

Does there need to be a sequence for each action?

Is this going to be part of a person's day job, or are they going to be given extra time?

When do you want it completed by?

Does it have to be done now, and what can be done later?

Have you built any unexpected delays into your timing?

Monitoring the actions

When the actions have been put in place, you need to monitor them to ensure that they are doing what was intended and stop those that are unsuccessful or those that are actually making the problem worse.

Monitoring is the process of continually assessing whether actions are achieving the Aim and Objectives. You will need to decide what information to collect; where from; how to collect it; who will collect it and when to collect it. The questions need to find out how things are going. Are they getting better, worse or staying the same? Is what we are doing making a difference? Are we still correct about what the problem is?

You will need to get a balance between measuring things to assess how things are going and measuring something just because you can. "You won't make a pig any bigger by keep weighing it!" I believe this statement was made by a Norfolk Police Officer, prompted after being monitored by an outside body.

Here is an example we can use, which follows a Problem Solving Process and shows how research, creative thinking and monitoring can lead to the modification of the action plan.

Nightclubs have a problem of people cutting their feet on broken glass, and the aim would be for this not to happen. The research tells you that women are being injured on the dance floor, after removing their shoes to dance more easily and then stepping on broken glass. The local hospital would share the problem, as well as the friends who would have to look after the injured.

Why is broken glass getting onto the dance floor? The answer is that people are carrying their glasses and bottles onto the dance floor with them as they dance. The glasses or bottles are then either put on the floor, where they are then kicked over, or they are dropped on the floor from peoples' hands while they are dancing.

The revised aim would be to stop glass getting onto the dance floor. You could tell people not to take the glasses and bottles onto the dance floor as they enter the club; when they buy their drinks; as they go onto the dance floor and by putting up signs around the club.

To find out the effect of these actions, you could monitor how many people took glasses onto the dance floor, how much broken glass was swept up and how many people were being injured every night.

After further thoughts, you may actually decide that the problem is the glass itself. Your revised aim would be "to have no breakable glass in the nightclub". There would also be a benefit that no other injuries would be caused by bottles and glasses during any fights. So, how can we go about eliminating broken glass from the night club? There are shatterproof glasses available, and good quality plastic glasses.

But what about the glass bottles? The suppliers could easily provide you with plastic bottles. Other customers, such as music event organisers, also share the problem, so there is a market for plastic bottles. However, here is the difficult bit. The producers of champagne do not have a plastic bottle alternative for you. You could stop serving champagne, but it is always in demand and you do make considerable profit from the sales.

This means that there is still a chance of the bottle breaking and glass getting onto the dance floor, or of it being used as a weapon. Do you have any thoughts? One idea was to put a deposit on the bottle to ensure that, once empty, it was returned to the bar. This was inspired from a time past when deposits were on bottles of lemonade which encouraged their return to the store. An early example of recycling.

How could this be monitored?

The amount of sales of champagne compared to sales before the deposit scheme. How many bottles were returned?

How many bottles of champagne ended up on the dance floor compared to how many before the scheme was started?

How many people were injured by being hit with champagne bottles. How many injures to women's feet?

A decision was made to introduce the deposit scheme. However, something unexpected happened. Other club members were taking the unattended champagne bottles from the table and collecting the deposit money themselves. As good practice, the deposit also had to be refunded to the person who had bought the champagne.

The next problem to overcome was how to ensure that the deposit was only returned to the right person and thereby negate the taking of other peoples Champagne bottles.

The latest method being used is to take the deposit using a credit card and then to reimburse the person on the return of the bottle, much like hotels do as a matter of course for their services.

Monitoring to confirm an action is effective

You will need to make sure that the things put into place are still there and being used correctly. An example of this was when concrete barriers were fitted to prevent disputes at cab ranks at an airport. A queuing system was in place but some cab driver would drive to the front of the queue, push in and encourage the travellers to take their cab. Something needed to be done as some of the disputes were resulting in fights between drivers. The concrete barriers were effective as they physically stopped mini cab drivers jumping the queue to collect the fares.

It also had a second benefit that customers, who may have been tempted to take advantage of the queue jumping cab drivers, could not physically get themselves and their luggage over the barriers. You need to make sure that the concrete blocks are still in place, and that the offending mini cabs have not overcome the obstacle and are again jumping the queue.

Monitoring to see if the action is achieving the aim

You need to make sure that those you are trying to change have not found a way around it. Just as an aside, people can be very creative at this point, and it is a shame they were not part of the session generating ideas.

An example of a tactic being negated is from Catalonia, Spain. A tactic used to put off sex workers trading alongside the road, was to fine sex workers working on the highway for not wearing fluorescent bibs as required by law. Two women were fined but now these women wear the yellow bibs and so this tactic is no longer effective.

Monitoring to make sure you have not made the situation worse

This is to check to make sure you are not making matters worse. An example was when a cleaning company, who had a contract to clean an underpass in Central London, had the problem of rough sleepers getting in the way of the cleansing machines. So the contractors decided to pay the few rough sleepers to go away when the machine arrived and save the crew time. Unfortunately, word got around that if you were in this subway at 7am you got paid to go away again. You have probably guessed already, and yes, the next day there were ten and by the end of the week over thirty. They stopped paying!

Additional points to be considered

How are you going to measure what's been done?

How does the person report any problems and give other feedback?

What system do you have in place if others are not doing as agreed? Ways of dealing with these providers needs to be established. The way it is to be done needs to be shared with those who are receiving the service.

If the plan is not being followed as expected, was the objective realistic or is there something wrong with the task?

Should more priority be placed on one or more of the objectives?

Reasons why your action plan may not be implemented

It's the problem   They do not share the problem

They do not appreciate the problem

It's the timing   It might be the wrong time, with other things taking place

What you are asking for is "ahead of the game". This is the situation where what you have suggested is so far ahead of the rest of the group that none can see the reason or benefit of what you foresee.

It's them   They are resistant to change

They are going soon and not interested

They get disillusioned while working on it

They did something like that before and it didn't work

They get bored and want to do something else more interesting

They can do it but it takes time and resources and they are too busy

It's you   It's not a good idea

They just don't like you!

Will the cure be worse than the problem?

There is going to be a point when you are ready to go ahead with your Action Plan but you are going to have to consider such things as risk assessment.

For example, in the 1930s the Australian sugar production was being affected by the cane beetle. This insect used to eat the young sugar cane causing damage to the plants. This was a problem and a solution was sought. The solution seemed ideal, the cane toad. In June 1935 they were imported from the Hawaiian Islands by the Bureau of Sugar Experiment Stations in an attempt to control the native cane beetle.

The toads were released into the cane fields with the intention that they would eat the beetle and solve the problem. Unfortunately, insufficient research was undertaken in the rush to implement the solution, which is something we examined earlier. The first bit of useful information was that cane toads cannot jump to the height of where the beetles lived. Fairly crucial really as that was going to be their core business.

We could think of a different solution here. Maybe they could have cross bred them with toads that were capable of jumping to the required height and then released them. Or you could just grow sugar beet!

Since their release, toads have rapidly multiplied in population and now number over **200 million** and have been known to spread diseases affecting local biodiversity. The cane toad competes with local frog species and due to its high toxicity kills any predator who preys on it, including snakes, raptors, lizards, and the Northern Quoll. (It's okay, I didn't know what it was either. The Northern Quoll is a small rodent).

Here are some attempts to resolve this 'cure'. In Queensland, Australia the government held the first 'Toad Day Out' where hundreds of locals went hunting for the invasive cane toad, catching an estimated 10,000 toads to be euthanized. Here is an evaluation undertaken by Professor Tony Peacock.

"Community groups have put in huge amounts of volunteer effort at hand-collecting toads and State governments also have put a lot of money into those activities. We admire the enthusiasm and commitment of the community groups. However, the physical removal can never stop the toad invasion. The reason is simple mathematics – to reduce the number of toads in an area, you have to take them out quicker than they can replace themselves. Cane toads reach maturity in just a few months, and a female can produce up to 30,000 eggs in a single clutch."

Well, it was an idea that captured the public imagination. Have you had any further thoughts on how to solve the problem?

There is some good news. See if this matched your idea: meat ants. Comparing habitat use and activity patterns of meat ants, cane toads, and seven native Australian frog species, researchers found that the cane toad was by far the most susceptible to predation by the meat ants.

Also, there is the lugworm, less dramatic but is seen to be effective.

Finally, it maybe that the cane toad is not the worst problem, it's just the most visible. In Australia nine natural species have actually been lost to the imported fox. Is it the demand that made toads the priority or the fact that people see the toads and not the foxes?

Making a risk assessment

If you are going to implement any actions, then you will need to do a risk assessment. For example, in one area of London they were having a problem of inconsiderate cyclists riding far too fast along some of their refurbished canal side paths. As a result, they commissioned the painting of realistic large holes on the path.

Cyclists seeing the image of the hole naturally slow down. To date no one has fallen into the canal but worth considering as part of a risk assessment.

Most Risk Assessment systems follow a basic four stage plan:

1. Identify the threats

What threats exist to affect or prevent your intervention from working?

What physical threats are there? Environmental? Natural? Human?

What technical threats are there? Procedural? IT failure?

What financial threats are there? Budget limits? Postponed funding?

Think about all the systems and structures you operate within your organisation and analyse risks to any part of them.

2. Estimate the risk

It is almost impossible to put a figure on risk. What is a minor risk for one person can be a major risk for another. One way of putting a figure on risk is to use this formula: Risk = probability of event x cost of event

3. Manage the risk

Once you have identified the threats and objectively calculated the level of risks, you can start looking at ways of managing them. It is important that you do not spend more money and resources to eliminate a problem than the current cost of the problem.

4. Review your assessment

Once you have carried out a risk assessment, it is worth carrying out regular reviews. The very action of putting interventions in place can change the nature of the risk. But not all risk assessment is about cost or potential injury. There is also the matter of whether your actions are infringing human rights and civil liberties. It is therefore worth learning a little about the legislation that governs such things.

An example of how the interventions were risk assessed, or not.

To help you with the way this system works let us look at an example, in this case the problem of dead whales ending up on beaches. Let us examine this problem and help us revise the problem solving approach so far.

Firstly, what is the problem?

Is the problem that the whales are beaching themselves and then dying, or are they already dead and the bodies are being washed up on the beach? You need to establish what your position is in relation to the problem. Are you an environmentalist, the Navy or the owner of the beach?

For this example we will look at the situation as if you were the Mayor of the coastal town and from time to time a dead whale appears on your beach. If you remember the Impact Scale, you cannot eliminate the whales dying, reduce their deaths or reduce the seriousness of the

---

injuries. Therefore you can only become more efficient at dealing with the consequence of the problem.

The problem is that you have a dead whale on your beach.

What aim shall be set?

Here are some choices. Do nothing and let nature takes its course. For your information, doing nothing will mean that the remains of the whale will enter the water and this in turn will attract sharks. The presence of the sharks will have a detrimental impact on tourism, which underpins your town's economy. So that's not going to be acceptable.

The aim therefore is to "Remove the whale from your beach" and, judging by the smell, by a certain time.

At this point you would ask the research questions such as, "What type of whale has beached, when did it arrive and what happened to cause it to be beached?" This information would be applicable if your aim was to prevent the whales from dying.

As your aim is to be "more efficient at dealing with the problem", then your questions will need to gather information that will help you make a judgement on what to do to get the whale off the beach. We would need to know the average number of beached whales we have a year in comparison with other beaches along the coastline. This in turn would help us decide on how much money would be set aside to resolve the problem.

For example, if there is a special winch that is used to move whales off the beach would it be a cost effective investment if we only get one beached whale every ten years?

You could even monitor the situation to determine if you actually get more tourists due to the whale and the appearance of the sharks. However, the people renting out the pedalos may not be so keen on that idea.

So far we have been looking at Convergent Research. The Divergent Research should be on finding others who have had the same, or a similar problem, to see if what they chose to do would be suitable for yourself.

Here is what happened when they moved a beached whale in Taiwan. The officials decided to undertake a post mortem and so loaded a beached whale onto a transporter to drive it to the place where it was to be done. Unfortunately, due to the condition of this particular whale, while it was being driven through a built up area, the whale's internal gases caused it to explode, projecting its decomposing body over fellow motorists and property. Therefore, although the idea of moving the whale could still be an option, the route would need to be carefully planned and an assessment made on the condition of the whale.

Time to have a think! An idea you may have is to move the whale away from the popular beach to one not visited, bury it or break it up and allow gulls to eat it.

Here was the situation for the coastal town of Florence, Oregon USA in 1970, when a sperm whale ended up dead on the beach. Let's see what we could learn about how to solve the problem and make risk assessments.

On Thursday, Nov 12, 1970, an 8-ton, 45-foot-long whale, dead for some time, washed up on the Pacific Ocean beach south of Florence, Oregon.

Because the Oregon beach is a public right of way, the State Highway Division was given the task of cleaning up the mess. Not the most logical choice, but these things happen.

Various ideas were considered but, if buried, the carcass would soon be uncovered by the ocean tides, and the time and effort would have been wasted.

It was a curiosity attraction for local residents and tourists. People took photos next to it, little kids crawled around on it, and the old whale was not an object of annoyance to anyone. But when the smell reached local homes, a decision was made to clean up the mess.

Cutting up the body was not an option – no one would want to deal with several tons of stinking, rotting meat.

So it was decided to blow it all up. The small pieces would then be picked up and eaten by crabs and gulls.

Officials at the Department of the Navy were consulted, and a plan was hatched to blast the blubber to smithereens, using a half-ton of dynamite. What little was left would be eaten by gulls. It reminds me of the quote that if you only have a hammer in your box, then you treat everything like a nail. What do the Navy do other than blow things up?

They decided to blow up the whale and, just to make sure, they added additional boxes of dynamite. When the explosives were detonated the spectators initially cheered but, in just a few moments, cheers turned into fearful screams as large chunks of rotten meat started falling from the sky.

A 3 x 5 foot piece of foul-smelling, rotting whale blubber had soared a quarter-mile through the air only to land on the top of a car, totally crushing it.

But the worst thing of all was that the smell of the rotten meat had increased tenfold and the gulls, which were supposed to eat the small chunks of meat, were nowhere to be found. Either they were scared away by the explosion, or they had flown away from the dreadful smell.

So, we learnt what happens when some sort of risk assessment is not applied, or when one is applied incorrectly.

Summary

We have looked at how the ideas become actions, how they can be applied, risk assessed and monitored. The next chapter looks at how we can measure whether what you and others have done has actually worked.

Chapter 6

Evaluation

The purpose of this chapter is to help you:

See if the aim has been met

Learn from your experiences

	Partnership Problem Solving Process
P	Problem and Partner Identification
A	Aim Setting
R	Research and Analysis
T	Thinking Creatively
N	Negotiating the Changes
E	**Evaluation**
R	Recognition and Reward
S	Sharing 'Good Practice'

Chapter 6

Evaluation

Introduction

At some point, you will need to know whether you have been successful in changing the situation and keeping it that way. There are two parts to this measurement, Impact Evaluation and Process Evaluation.

Impact Evaluation - Did it work?

Whenever people present a problem and all the things they and others have done, there is a killer question that will come up and one that everyone poses which is "Well did it work?" For example, the strap line on a number of commercially available diet plans state that "the weight goes and stays off". The emphasis on the "stays off" has come about as a result of comments like "this diet is all very well to lose weight but then it all goes back on again".

Questions you need to ask yourself

1   Was the aim met? If not, why not?

2   Did my actions cause the change?

3   Did the change make it worse for someone else?

Was the aim met? If not, why not?

Either the aim was or was not met. To help you with this, you need to make use of the baseline. The baseline was the measurement you took when you researched your problem. As a reminder, it was a 'snapshot' of where you were at the start so that you had data to measure your success against. It is a description of the situation at the start of a problem solving initiative before any work has been carried out.

For example, you may have wanted to increase sales and had chosen to do it by launching an extensive mail shot, encouraging people to visit your website and in turn place an order for your product or service. You would want to know if there had been an increase in the number of hits on your company website as a result of your promotion.

Therefore, you could use two baselines.

The first measure would be how many hits you were getting on your website before your mail shot went out.

The second baseline would be how many of those hits had previously been converted to a sale.

Your evaluation would then be all about measuring whether you had an increase in hits during the campaign and also how many of those hits converted to sales. One method to distinguish the regular hits, from those resulting from the mail shot is to provide the customer with a code. The code would be given to provide a discount. This would then identify them as someone prompted by the mail shot.

How to undertake your Impact Evaluation

Who should do the evaluation?

Preferably anyone other than yourself or your team, as people will not believe that you will be impartial, especially if what you did was a great success. People may doubt the way you collected the data. For example I was invited to assess the performance of the front counter staff. A survey had been conducted to measure customer satisfaction.

However, the survey forms had only been given to those who were happy with the service. Anyone who was not satisfied was never given a form.

When should it be done?

At the end of the initiative. This should have been described in the aim. For example," by.....date the following will have been achieved".

What is going to be measured?

We have to make sure that we have not "hit the target but missed the point" This focus on specifics has become the bane of Problem Solving, where efforts made to measure something result in the wrong thing being measured, which then creates activity to hit the measure as opposed to actions that are in place to meet the long term aim.

Evaluations can be made using Quantitative and Qualitative measures.

Quantitative data involves numbers

You can count such measures before and after your actions, and note the difference. Quantitative measures allow you to use statistics to estimate the impact of your action. An example could be the decrease in graffiti in a certain area.

Qualitative data relates to opinions and feelings

Qualitative data is generally harder to gather than quantitative data but can often be more revealing. For example, how did you feel about the way a cashier handled your purchase. The answer, however, is normally converted to a quantitative measure to enable the results to be compared over time. For example, "from 1 to 5, 1 being the lowest, how well did the sales assistant appear to understand your needs?"

Contact the people who made the demand

When we undertook our Research we needed to find the people, department or organisation who were making the demand for something to be done about a problem. What they wanted and why it was important to them was covered in your Research of the Problem.

When undertaking the Qualitative Evaluation, I strongly recommend that you make sure that the people who made the demand are interviewed.

Make sure they are happy about the new situation. There is a chance that they are not approached at the end of your initiative. Yet the issue was raised by them in the first place and it would be best to verify with them that the problem has been resolved. The questions could be based on comparisons, for example "Compared to the situation last year, are things better, the same or worse?"

If these were customers, what a smart move for a company to get them to confirm all is well. Otherwise, they may have moved on to new issues and, assuming you had done nothing, may tell other people how poorly you had performed.

Give these same people, who had made the demand, details of people or departments to contact if the problem emerges again. If you are able to give them a reference that would be ideal, as those employed to work on the problem may have changed.

Did my actions cause the change?

There may have been other influences that occurred which had an impact on your problem.

For example, a Police Force in the UK had a dramatic reduction in cars being broken into over the year. An evaluation took place to see what had been done. The reason for the reduction was that it was the year Foot and Mouth disease had broken out and a National Park in their area had been closed. The car parks within this National Park had always accounted for a large number of the yearly car crimes, but as there were no tourists, there were no cars to steal from. The crime figures went back up after a while, when the car park was reopened.

Was the problem solved or displaced?

The question of whether a problem is actually solved or just displaced is a valid question and one you need to consider and measure. For example, it could be that a problem of pollution was resolved because higher chimneys were built to disperse the soot.

Let us look at Crime Prevention for information to help us consider how problems can be displaced. Displacement Theory argues that removing opportunity for crime or seeking to prevent a crime by changing the situation in which it occurs, does not actually prevent crime but merely moves it around. There are five main ways in which this theory suggests crime is moved around:

1 crime can be moved from one **location** to another
2 crime can be moved from one **time** to another
3 crime can be directed away from one **target** to another
4 one **method** of committing crime can be substituted for another
5 one **kind of crime** can be substituted for another
   (Felson and Clarke, 1998)

Considering these points, we need to ask questions about our own problem. Has our problem just moved? For example, has the congestion at our hotel moved from one location to another point? Has the problem moved to a different time, so the congestion moves from one time to another, as opposed to getting any less?

Process Evaluation

This is a review of what else went on. It means looking back over the work done and, regardless of results, asking some questions:

What went well? Why did it go well?

What didn't go well? Why not?

What could be done better next time?

What would I never do again?

Feedback is a gift...though not always welcomed

You need to remember that not everyone will want to receive your feedback, however tempting it is to share it. As an advisor I always have to tread carefully when offering feedback. If you are able to give your feedback, make sure it is something they can actually use, and always balance negative with positive comments. Also seek feedback from them about something you have done as well, including how you gave your feedback.

Everyone's a winner

Unfortunately, most projects always appear to be a success. That's the way of the world. But important learning is not always captured and shared. Or if it is, then it's done privately, so you will need to get the trust of those involved in sharing with you what did not go well.

Reasons why problems fail to be resolved

Even though this book is about Problem Solving and thereby making a positive difference, we need to accept it does not always happen. Even though I specialise in Problem Solving, I am not always successful. When this happens I reflect on why that occurred. Was it something I did, something others did, or that other factors were present or were not present to cause it to fail?

I have found a number of reasons why Problem Solving does not work. Some are out of the control of the people working on the problem, while others are down to the people themselves. I have divided these reasons into two parts, ones from outside the group and ones from inside the group.

External factors out of the control of the individual or group

The problem is just too big

This is when people take on a problem which is frankly just too big for them to address or that the time period is too short in which to resolve it. It sometimes happens when the task has been given by someone who has either underestimated the scale of the problem or overestimated the ability of the person or partnership tasked to address it.

Being given a problem to work on, but not in a position to progress the actions required to resolve it

The person or group may have been given someone else's problem to work on but are obliged to hand back the action plan to be progressed by them. In this situation, the solutions may not be sustained.

An example of this situation is where a young man had been offered a place at a popular University, known to have a shortage of rooms in the halls of residence, which were allocated on a 'first come, first served' basis. He had very specific requirements with regard to the location and facilities of the accommodation, so he asked his mother to perform the research required to solve this problem. After spending time surfing the appropriate web sites, his mother identified the ideal situation and gave her son the details for the application form. You have guessed it! Because he was absorbed in planning his trip to a music festival, the young man failed to promptly submit the application form and so failed to secure his required accommodation. Learning did take place!

There is external pressure to do something quickly

This pressure can be within the group or from the group's leader, but it is normally from the person who gave out the problem to be resolved. I appreciate why this is done when the effects of the problems are serious or when those making the demands are very influential. However, this intense pressure to do something can result in people not having an opportunity to think about the problem and just end up doing some sort of activity to appease those seeking an instant remedy. There is also a risk that there is not the structure or enough resources in place to support the actions when there is pressure to do something quickly.

Not enough resources

This is when the aim chosen for the group to work towards is not followed up with enough resources to support any actions required, or the people working on it do not have the time to do so. It may be that they had time to start with but were then given further tasks. I have seen processes that are good at asking people about their problems but that do not have the capacity to effectively work on them. Sometimes, actions are started with not enough resources available to sustain them.

Setting the actions for another

I have seen Strategic Groups, who were too far away from the problem, but still set the solutions. This is not the best method as it can result in the people tasked with the actions, resenting them. Therefore, instead of working on the problem, they spend their time proving why the proposals are wrong. A better approach is to have discussions between those from the Strategic Group and those who have the responsibility of implementing the actions, described as the practitioners. This enables the sharing of all information, together with a mutual understanding of the demands on everyone and the difficulties connected with implementing the actions.

It's not a problem!

Just because someone tells you it is a problem, however emotionally charged up they are about it, does not make it so. This situation is all too common in Problem Solving and detracts people and resources from working on genuine problems.

It starts with a person mistakenly deciding that something is a problem. (This is different from the situation where people talk up a problem, as at least one exists, which was covered earlier in the book.) They make a point of telling others, lots of others, lots of times and the higher up the chain the better. These people can be very passionate, articulate and persuasive. They will identify and approach a number of people, including the legal system or the media, to further their case.

A consequence of the strength of their own belief, is that they can convince others of the severity of the problem and that nothing of value is being done. All this makes it very hard for the person dealing with it to resolve the issue or to give the complainant a reality check!

These people exist in the legal world and they are the people that start court proceedings against others. They are described as vexatious litigators. These vexatious people are the problem!

How a vexatious person can be managed

Have only one person from the organisation or partnership to be their single point of contact (SPOC). In that way, people are not played off against each other, or trapped into making unsolicited comments.

Investigate thoroughly each point raised. This can take hours, but it is good investment because, if the complaint is genuine, then you can work on resolving the problem. Also, this means that you are fully aware of the problem and what has been done so far, so you can ensure that your organisation is not vulnerable to criticism and is better placed to cope with future litigation. If you believe the problem to be false or exaggerated, then the in depth questioning will highlight this.

The complaints sometimes come as letters but most often as an email. I describe them as 'soufflé letters' as the person creating them, has taken the existing material and then rigorously whisked it up into something that looks far more substantial than it actually is and, just like a soufflé, it is very vulnerable to collapse when pressure, e.g. questioning, is applied.

When it has been established that nothing further can be done, someone with authority within the organisation needs to confirm this. Then the complainant needs to be contacted to have the position explained and be told clearly that nothing further will be done. A good knowledge of Customer Care would be very useful when you have reached this stage.

Internal factors within the control of the individual or the group

People become too emotionally involved

Some people, quite understandably, become emotionally involved in the problem. That's great when there is a need for passion to drive through the changes needed. However, those involved sometimes set unrealistic aims, both in the target and the time scale in which the Problem Solving initiative needs to be completed by.

They sometimes over promise to others which then makes it harder to placate these same people later when the sheer magnitude of the problem has been found or when the resources are not available to deal with it. I was once at a public meeting where the senior person present got so caught up in the event that he invited people in the audience, faced with unresolved problems, to phone him and then promptly gave out his mobile number. It was not long before he changed his phone!

People are not methodical when dealing with a complex problem

This is when someone, or a group set up to work on a problem, does not have a systematic approach to defining the problem and researching it, but starts to act without appreciating why certain Problem Solving stages or processes are in place. In fact, a process may be in place to prevent a problem that had occurred previously. However, I do appreciate the pressures to do something, and it could be that you make a decision to move on, knowing the risks.

For example, in World War 2, when the Allies landed on the beaches of Normandy they needed a way of landing both men and materials efficiently. Two mobile harbours were constructed on the beach, named Mulberry 1 and 2.

One was for the Americans and one was for the British and Canadians. Because time was crucial in getting as much material and as many men ashore as possible, the Americans took a series of short cuts, such as not anchoring the harbour to the sea bed.

The British and Canadians, instead, followed the processes correctly and it took far longer to become operational. So, in the short term, credit goes to the Americans.

However, a severe storm broke out and hit both the American and British Harbours. The American one broke up while the British one survived. Now credit goes to the British and Canadian long term approach.

On this occasion, the Allies were able to take advantage of both approaches by running the projects side by side, which is something you may need to do with your problem. The challenge is to make sure that the short term actions are not detrimental to the long term action plan.

People take over someone else's problem solving work

This is when people work on a problem which is not theirs to lead. Often, those who should take the lead in tackling a problem fail to take any action and the work is passed onto others who, unfortunately, have to deal with the consequences. In other cases it is either because people want to expand their own influence, or to have access to other budgets. But in the end, it is not a sustainable situation.

People jump to a solution

This is when people set up to work on a problem do not spend much time, if any, on trying to define the problem. Instead, they leap to a solution as if they are on some 'murder mystery weekend' with only a short time to solve it. This can result in them working on the wrong problem or where the chosen actions will not make any difference to it. At best it can be described as an activity, but it's not Problem Solving.

Not making use of tools and techniques

There are many tools and techniques available to analyse a problem and to generate ideas to resolve it. Not knowing what is available and how to use them will hamper progress in understanding the analysis and limit the number of different ways you use to resolve the problem.

People jump to their favourite solution

This is when people use the same response to everything, without considering whether it is still the best option. It's just their favourite action. The justification they give is that "we have always done it that way". That's great, but if it's still the best way, it can survive a small amount of testing to see if it is still fit for purpose or if there are other, better ways to do something.

Ideas that fail to support the objective or aim

This is when everyone falls in love with the idea, and carries on with it, without considering whether it supports the aim. Maybe you have watched a TV advert and, though impressed with it, are still none the wiser as to what they are selling or even the company who have funded it, something I thought an advert was meant to do.

Only proven ideas are accepted

This is when new ideas are rejected as there is no previous evidence to show that it had worked before. This is known as an 'evidence based approach. This restricts the trialing of new ideas.

People miss opportunities of working with others

These could be those who have first hand experience of the problem and for some reason are not included in trying to resolve it. These people could even be the ones making the complaints in the first place.

Being distracted

This is the situation when someone or a group gets distracted by something presented to them. The result is that the research of the problem is curtailed along with any more meaningful actions that will address the problem. If the solutions are rather mundane in nature, they are set aside in favour of the more attractive option.

Scorched earth approach

I have used this term to describe a far too common response to a problem. Scorched earth is a military strategy or operational method which involves destroying anything that might be useful to the enemy. So instead of dealing with the problem, people become fixated on something that is present and remove it, believing that will clear the problem.

For example, when people are causing anti social behaviour and are sometimes gathering on nearby benches, it is a far too common action to just to remove the bench, irrespective that other people need the benches, such as the elderly. This means an amenity used by others is taken away. If disorderly people are taking advantage of the position to view and abuse passersby, then maybe you could turn the bench to face the other way. This opposite, or reverse thinking, was looked at earlier in the book.

Poor implementation of a good solution

This is when the Problem Solving Process has been applied correctly and an effective solution has been developed but then not implemented correctly.

For an example to support this I need to mention one of the greatest problem solvers in the 20th Century, Major- General Percy Hobart. There is so much about his life and work that demonstrates his Problem Solving ability but for brevity I will only focus on one area of his work, which is where he and the 79th Armoured Division overcame a specific problem set by the German army in World War 2.

In 1944 the Germans were anticipating an invasion from the Allies, somewhere along the coastline of Western Europe. The desire of the German commanders was to defeat the enemy on the beaches, and they set about devising problems for the men and tanks landing on the shore. Major-General Hobart and his men invented a range of tanks to overcome the problems set by the Germans. He had tanks equipped with flails that rotated in front of them, setting off the mines to clear a path for the people and vehicles following behind.

To overcome the problem of ditches, some tanks had bridges fixed onto their vehicle, while others dropped bundles of material into the gaps. To overcome the encased bunkers, a huge mortar was created that was projected onto the bunker.

One of the most impressive inventions was to adapt tanks so that they could travel through the water, land on the beach and start fighting.

Each tank had a water proof cover fitted around the tank and a propeller fitted, which enabled it to be launched into the water some way back from the beach. The tank would then travel through the water onto the beach and, once there, the collar dropped away and the tank crew could engage the enemy. It worked.

What happened next is why I use this example to explain why Problem Solving sometimes fails due to poor execution of the solution. The Americans at Omaha beach launched their adapted tanks too far out, and so beyond what could be reasonably expected from the water proof collar. Also, it is believed that these brave tank drivers themselves turned them slightly sideways towards their intended beach. This decision unfortunately only increased the amount of water getting over the collar and they all sunk. This meant that the tanks failed to get to the shore to support the troops landing on the beach.

Percy Hobart is certainly worth studying to see how he overcame problems he faced and how he was valued by some and dismissed by others. He was knighted by King George VI. The Americans awarded him the Legion of Merit, Degree of Commander. He is a great role model for Problem Solvers.

Summary

We have looked at the crucial role Evaluation plays in Problem Solving to confirm what works; what does not work so well; what does not work at all and the possible reasons for failure. In effect, this is the end of a Problem Solving Process, but there is also Good Practice and the next two Chapters look at the need to reward people and how you can share what you have learnt.

Who shares your problem?
_____

Chapter 7

Recognition and Reward

The purpose of this chapter is to help you:

Appreciate the need to recognise others

Identify who to recognise and ways how to do it

Partnership Problem Solving Process	
P	Problem and Partner Identification
A	Aim Setting
R	Research and Analysis
T	Thinking Creatively
N	Negotiating the Changes
E	Evaluation
R	**Recognition and Reward**
S	Sharing 'Good Practice'

Chapter 7

Recognition and Reward

Introduction

I have visited a number of people who have successfully made changes, some recognised and some not. The ones recognised proudly tell me what happened and sometimes show me a Certificate or another form of recognition. You can tell that if they were asked to work on something else they would have the same level of commitment.

I have also found others who had shown commitment and self sacrifice and had not been recognised. It is hard to say whether they would approach the next task with the same level of enthusiasm as before and what is so sad is that all they really wanted was some sort of recognition. Some still would, because that's the way they are, but you risk losing others.

Who could you recognise?

Those who raised it as a problem

These are the people we identified in the research stage who had made the demand for something to be done. For example, if a number of complaints had come in about your product, these people will have given you the knowledge that something was going wrong. What a great group of people to be there monitoring how things are going and how better than to thank them for raising the issues. They will certainly tell you what is really happening, and in time could become your great advocates instead of telling people how bad you are.

Those who were interviewed about the problem

These are the people who had spent their time being interviewed by you about the problem. It would be good to thank them. It may even be that the person you thanked provides you with further information about the problem, which had not come out at the time of the interview.

Those you visited to see what they had done

These people not only gave up their time, but also gave useful information about how they solved a problem similar to your own. As I mentioned above, a thank you or token of your appreciation would be a good thing to do as it may be they have had further progress on the problem and now feel motivated to tell you more about these developments. It would really strengthen your partnership. I have found that this policy of reward and recognition is particularly well used in the USA.

Those who implemented your actions

For these people it may not have been an easy task for them, and a thank you would be a good thing. It may be that, as you have taken time to thank them, they in turn take time to give you feedback on what was good and what could have been done better. In the same way, they may even have thought of other ways that things could have been done to address your problem.

Those who were interviewed at the Evaluation stage

These people took time to tell you whether the problem had been resolved and what could have been done better. After you have thanked them they may feel better disposed towards you and give you further information that could be useful. However, only do it after you get the feedback or you may influence the results.

Recognition is its own Reward

Go and see them and say thank you.

Send them a thank you card.

Send them a letter. There's nothing quite as nice as opening a 'thank you' letter that acknowledges your efforts. (A way to write one is in the Appendix 1)

Send a separate letter to their line manager.

Send them an email and cc their line manager. The cc means that others can see what they have done without them appearing to be self promoting.

Mention them and what they did in their internal newsletter and on the organisation website

Send an article including details of them to your trade magazine.

Mention what they did to the media. Local newspapers or radio stations are always looking for good news stories and really like the fact that it is a local company or organisation.

Give them a financial reward.

Give them paid time off work

Offer them a training course. (maybe a one day Refresher Problem Solving course by Sixth Sense)

Fund (or part fund) a qualification.

Allow an attachment or secondment.

Run a competition

If you are interested, we at Sixth Sense have details of our Problem Solving competition called 'PARTNERS' Problem Solving and Partnership Awards, that you can have free of charge. Just email admin@sixthsensetraining.co.uk and ask for the information. Naturally, we would like to be recognised when you hold an event.

Summary

We have looked at why it is beneficial to thank others and how to do it.

When you are looking at praiseworthy work, it would be a good thing to share your 'Good Practice' with others. This next chapter looks at how this could be done.

Who shares your problem?

Chapter 8

Sharing 'Good Practice'

The purpose of this chapter is to help you:

Appreciate the benefits of sharing 'Good Practice'

Share 'Good Practice' in a number of ways

Partnership Problem Solving Process	
P	Problem and Partner Identification
A	Aim Setting
R	Research and Analysis
T	Thinking Creatively
N	Negotiating the Changes
E	Evaluation
R	Recognition and Reward
S	**Sharing 'Good Practice'**

Chapter 8

Sharing 'Good Practice'

Introduction

As you have seen from earlier parts of the book, once you have defined your problem and set your aim, you investigate other ways the problem has been tackled and identify the good and bad practice of others. Hopefully, you would have benefitted from the work of others. This chapter is about how you, in turn, can help others to make changes for the better.

Within your organisation

Add a section on 'Sharing Good Practice' into internal staff appraisals on how the person identified and applied the good practice of others.

You could phrase questions in their review as follows:

"Do you look at your colleagues and identify their good practice?"
"Have you visited others to see what good practice is available?"
"Can you demonstrate changes you have made as a result of observing the good practice of others?"

Add 'Sharing Good Practice' as an agenda item for your team meetings.

Add a section on 'Sharing Good Practice' to internal inspections or within self assessments.

Implement a suggestion scheme.

Create a 'Good Practice' data base.

Post up examples of 'Good Practice' on the website.

Place an article in your internal newsletter.

Outside your organisation

Attend conferences and present your 'Good Practice' to others.

Arrange your own conferences for the purpose of sharing 'Good Practice' within a certain profession.

Write articles in newspapers or trade magazines.

Post your reports and work on websites.

Contribute your work to specific publications.

Deliver presentations to others.

Presentations

If you and your partnership have developed 'Good Practice', people will want to come to see what you did and learn from you. Although this is very rewarding and being recognised is something people like, it can have its downside. I have seen a number of projects that slow down as the practitioners spend most of their time providing briefings, taking phone calls and managing visits.

Therefore, I recommend the following:

Have a briefing report written and posted onto your internet site.

Provide an email address for people to send questions or contact you. Remember that the problem being faced may be where the world time difference makes it difficult for them to contact you.

Host a discussion forum at a time and place suitable for you, where you can answer questions. In that way you do not have to break up the rest of your time with individual visits. You could then take the opportunity of getting feedback on your work from others as well as getting their ideas and experiences to learn from.

Consider hosting an internet conference.

Conclusion

I do hope that this book has been informative and will help you in tackling your own problems and in working with others who share your problem.

You can always email me with your thoughts, ideas and experiences. Hey, I might even know someone who shares your problem.

Best regards
Neil Henson

neilhenson@sixthsensetraining.co.uk

Here is a problem before you go...

You are a farmer and your sheep are getting out of the field and onto the road, causing traffic problems and a risk of injury to the animals. You have checked your fences and they are secure. You do not have a gate, because you have a cattle grid in place to stop the sheep from walking out of the entrance.

A friend tells you that he has heard that sheep have learnt to roll over the cattle grid to avoid the gaps.

So what are you going to do next?

For the answer to this please go to our website
www.sixthsensetraining.co.uk

Acknowledgements

Ian Barber, Simon Cham, Steve Colgan, Gerald Connor, Gary Cordner, John Eck, Justin Fahy, Audrey Helps, Katya Henson, Sarah Henson, Justin Hulford, Kerry Hutton, Joe Kettle, Paul King, Brian Livesey, Anne MacDonald, Gil Martin, Mark Parry, Tony Peacock, Mark See, Mike Scott, Paul Scott, Mark Scoular, Susan Smith, Sam Spencer, Aimee Summers, Michael Summers, Bob Thomson, Mike Ward, Deborah Wates, Andy Whitfield, Chris Williams, Lee Wollaston, Eve Woodroofe...and all the problem solvers who have shared with me their successes and setbacks.

Designed and produced for print and Kindle by Butler Systems Design Limited. www.butlersystems.com

Appendices

1. How to write a Problem Solving Letter

2. How to hold a Problem Solving Meeting

3. How to write a Problem Solving Report

4. How to deliver a Problem Solving Presentation

5. PARTNERS A Problem Solving Process

Appendix 1

How to write a Problem Solving Letter

In these days of text messaging and email, letter writing seems to be a dying art. However, a well-constructed and precisely worded letter can achieve extraordinary results. As I said earlier in the book, you could use a letter for thanking people, as well using letters for doing research or getting funding for one of your actions.

Before you start, decide what you want to say and make a list of the points you want to include;

Arrange your points in a logical order

Use a separate paragraph for each point

Quote any references, contact names, addresses, telephone numbers or email addresses

Don't waffle and don't tell the reader what they already know

The header

Give the letter a heading so that your reader will know what the letter is about as soon as they open it. Don't use ALL UPPER CASE letters or underline as this makes things difficult to read. **Bold** is much better.

The content

Use Plain English

Use punctuation to help clarity and understanding

Use short, simple sentences

If the letter covers different subjects, consider giving each one a new heading

Consider numbering the paragraphs if this will help the reader

Be brief. Long letters don't get read. Aim for one side of A4

If you have to include lots of information, consider using appendices

Quote references, telephone numbers etc.

The tone

Your tone will let your reader know what your attitude is toward them. Aim for a tone that will achieve the desired result. Don't use ambiguous words and phrases. Be appropriate, tactful, helpful, polite, sympathetic and honest.

Opening and closing

Informal address:
"Dear Mr/Mrs/Ms" and end with "Yours sincerely." (Of course, use of a first name is appropriate if you know the reader)

Formal address:
"Dear Sir/Madam" and end with "Yours faithfully."

Checklist

Does your first paragraph introduce the subject of your letter?

If you're replying to a letter, have you thanked the person for their letter? It is courteous and does not admit liability.

Does your final paragraph summarise the letter and point the way ahead?

Have any important facts been left out?

Is there too much detail? If so, what? Get rid of the waffle!

Having read your letter, will your reader know what they need to do, or what you are going to do?

If you get the opportunity, get someone else to read through your letter. If time is not pressing, then email it to them to read and give feedback on what they liked and did not like.

Appendix 2

How to hold a Problem Solving Meeting

At some point, it is going to make sense for all those who share the problem to gather together at a meeting. However, meetings don't have a very good reputation, do they? And yet, meetings are one of the most powerful and effective ways of getting business done if...and this is a very big 'if', they are planned and run correctly.

So, how many meetings do you attend that are properly planned? How many are rambling and aimless? How many meetings have you been to where it's obvious that the wrong people are there, and the people who should be there aren't there? And, be honest, ... how many of your own meetings have gone completely to plan?

What is a meeting?

The purpose of an effective meeting is to achieve a set of objectives in the minimum time to the satisfaction of the participants.

Led by a Chair (person), the participants will;

discuss a set agenda of items (objectives)

decide actions

record discussions and actions (the minutes)

decide who will do them

This definition may seem a little rigid, but just think for a moment about some of the dreadful meetings that you've been to. What was wrong with them? Would they have been better if the organiser had stuck to our definition?

What you need to consider when holding a meeting?

Why hold a meeting? Can the content or information be passed on in another way i.e. memo, e-mail, face-to-face, briefing etc.?

Who should you invite? Are they the right people? Can they offer anything constructive? Are you inviting the purse holder or the spender? Who shouldn't you invite?

What is the purpose of the meeting? What do you hope to gain from holding it?

When should you hold the meeting? Is the time and date suitable for all? Does it clash with other important business? Are there deadlines to meet? Have you considered the workloads of those you are inviting?

Where should you hold the meeting? Can everybody get there? Is the location suitable for the size of the group? Is it suitable for anyone with a disability? Do you need a hearing loop? Does the venue have the resources you'll need? Could you hold it somewhere relevant to the items being discussed so that participants can see the issues first-hand?

How should you hold your meeting, over breakfast or lunch? What style is appropriate, formal or less formal? Will the style distract participants from the business in hand? Will the Chair be able to keep control? Will the layout of the venue or seating plan be appropriate?

DID – Discussion, Information, Decision

Another way of asking the question "Do I need to hold a meeting?" is to use the DID Formula, either to the purpose of the meeting, or the objectives within it.

Discussion

Is there a more time-effective and cost-effective way of having a discussion? If all you're doing is looking at options but not coming to any conclusion (such as generating ideas or brainstorming), could this be done without getting everyone together e.g. by e-mail or questionnaire?

Information

If all you need to do is assign tasks or share information, hold a quick briefing instead. In fact, a memo or a few short phone calls may be an even more effective use of your time and everybody else's time. Meetings are about participation and shared decision-making. No participation required = no meeting required.

Decision

If decisions are needed, a meeting may be required. But only if the people invited to the meeting have some say in the decision making process. If decisions are unilateral, there is no need for a meeting. You just need to pass on the relevant information.

Planning your Meeting

Stage 1 - Purpose

Be clear why you need a meeting. Be clear what your objectives are. List the topics. It may be to define the problem or agree on an aim.

Stage 2 - Let people know

Make sure everyone knows what is being discussed - create an agenda. Make it clear why you want a meeting and what you want from it. Anticipate who might be needed and what information. They might need research already gathered on the problem.

Select the right participants. Select the Chair (if not chairing personally). Ensure that everyone can attend, or can at least send a deputy who, if possible, has been given authority to make some, or all, of the decisions.

Stage 3 - Prepare the order

Prepare a logical sequence of items on the agenda. Base the time allowed for each item on importance, not urgency. It may be you start with a video clip of the problem. I have found this is a very effective way of conveying the problem and focusing on the problem.

However, it may also stimulate solutions. These ideas should be captured, but make sure the meeting doesn't change to one where those solutions are started without further thought to the research about the problem, or the consequences to others of a solution being chosen and implemented.

Stage 4 - Control it

Introduce the subject of the meeting - Explain why the meeting is necessary. Explain the current position and what you want to achieve or change. Plan the discussion - Involve all group members, encourage contribution. Participation - What would participants suggest? Draw out and examine current situation, peoples' experiences and ideas. Find solution(s) and appoint people to actions.

Stage 5 - Summarise the points and record them

Summarise, clarify and agree options/actions.
Conclude meeting - Thank participants, confirm what actions will be taken, by whom and when. Arrange date of next meeting if you need one.

What goes on the agenda?

Title of meeting. Date, time, venue

The purpose of the meeting

Apologies for absence

Minutes of previous meeting

Items to be discussed and decided

Motions related to the above

Reports from sub-committees and thematic groups

Contributions from guest speakers

Date, time and venue of next meeting

Use verbs ('doing' words) in your agenda items. Agenda items should always be 'active' in order to focus the participants on the task in hand. Remember that a meeting relies on participation and 'doing' something.

An agenda item that says:

'Item 1: Budgets'
This means nothing in itself and time will be wasted in having to explain what the item means. It's far more effective to explain the agenda item more fully and to use verbs to show the activity required.

'Item 1: Discuss the forthcoming annual budget so that heads of departments may submit their applications for extra funding if required.'
It's significantly longer but, if I were attending the meeting, I'd know precisely why I'd been invited and would be able to prepare myself with facts, figures or maybe even a presentation.

Choosing a venue

The appropriate venue is critical to a good meeting. That doesn't mean that you have to get the best, most expensive room that you can, or that the furniture is of the highest standards (although such things can help).

It means choosing a site that is:

Convenient for participants.

Light and spacious, well-ventilated and not too hot or too cold.

Refreshments – even if all you have available is water.

Disabled access and hearing loops.

Never overcrowd your room or your table.

The Chair should occupy a position that gives them some degree of authority.

Hold a pre-meeting meeting

Both the Chair and Minute takers can benefit from having a short get-together before the meeting starts. The following topics can be usefully discussed:

Technical terminology. If the minute taker is unfamiliar with any of the terminology to be used, the chairperson can explain some of the words or terms most likely to arise. It may be useful to provide a glossary.

Structure of the meeting. The chairperson can explain to the minute taker how they intend to chair the meeting. This will aid the note-taking.

Type of minute needed. Ask the chairperson of the type of minutes needed, i.e. - action notes, verbatim record, threads of discussion and decisions etc. Survey those who receive them - how are they used?

Summarising. Ask the Chairperson to summarise each item to make the note taking easier.

Interrupting. The minute taker can establish the acceptability of interrupting the meeting if unsure of what to note; to remind the chair of timing or to remind the chair to summarise. Co-operation between the chairperson and the minute taker is essential to the success of meetings and will avoid lengthy drafting and re-drafting of minutes.

How to conduct the meeting

State the **purpose** of the meeting.

Open the meeting in a friendly manner.

Allow people to re-orientate themselves before tackling the main task.

Give an introductory statement summarising what is known, what is required and how you wish to tackle it.

Start discussion on each item and avoid old ground. Keep members to the point and check for misunderstandings.

Be aware of the needs of the group and of individuals. Draw out the silent and control the ones who dominate the conversations.

Prevent private discussion in splinter groups.

Discourage the clash of personalities, but encourage discussion of differing ideas.

The Chair must listen. Too much talk from the Chair stifles the participation of members.

Summarise often, to bring discussion back to the point and to close each item.

Thank individual and group contributions.

Final summary – confirm conclusions, clarify the actions and who is to lead them.

Appendix 3

How to write a Problem Solving Report

Make it as short as possible

Make it understandable after just one read

Get to the point without waffling

Leave the reader in no doubt as to what it is telling them/asking for

How many reports do you see that fit all four criteria? And, be honest, how many reports have you written that fit all four criteria? Most reports we see are badly constructed, rambling, overly long and far too complicated. Plus, there is a myth that adding complex words adds 'weight' to a report. No it doesn't. It just makes the report harder to read and therefore, less likely to get progressed.

Which report are you going to look at first: the four page report written in Plain English or the 80 page report written in gobbledegook? Incredibly, both reports may actually be asking for the same thing.

Plan your report

Too often report writers skip over this stage and proceed straight to the report. What happens then is a rambling journey around the subject, with occasional hints at the topic. Would you attempt a journey to somewhere new without planning it and just hope that you will 'get there in the end'? I doubt it. Would you attempt to build a house without planning it? Of course you wouldn't. So how can you hope to build a good report without planning?

It doesn't take very long to do, but the rewards are huge. Your report will stay focussed on the purpose and you'll know where you're going. Once you've planned the content, structure the report.

First, you need to know what to 'build' and for whom:

Who is it for?

Why do they want it?

What do you want to achieve by writing it?

Then you assemble the 'parts' you need:

Research the topic.

Decide on the items you want to include.

Group related items together.

Get rid of anything irrelevant or repetitive.

Now you have a plan – the blueprint for your report – you need a structure to build upon.

Here is one format of a report.

Purpose (Why you are writing this report)

I use this one to describe the reason or purpose for the report. It should only be about one or two sentences. I find it helps me to focus the report, to confirm with the person commissioning the report that it covers the areas they want and to provide clarity for the reader.

Situation (What is the position at the moment)

The second paragraph sets the scene, but does not describe the problem.

Problem (What's wrong with this position)

The third and following paragraphs describe each problem. If the report is about more than one problem, then each one needs to be isolated, and I suggest giving a letter to each one. (You should save numbers for the options for each one). You could use a a sketch plan, and add to it as you explain the problem, or have a series of sketches or photographs.

Options (What is available to improve the situation)

The next section is about what could be done, described as the options. (Remember, one option is to do nothing but monitor the situation). You may have a preferred one, but you need to give the reader a choice of options, as it demonstrates that you have the capability of considering other options, and maybe yours is not the right one.

Against each option, you should outline the positives and negatives. If you have more than one problem then each one needs to be identified and the options listed and numbered under each one.

Proposal (What is the best option and why)

The final section features the option you prefer. It is not unreasonable for you to state which one you think is the best option.

Putting together the report

Make your report look like something someone would want to read. Japanese cookery has an old adage: *The first bite is with the eye,* meaning that food will be more appetising if it looks appetising. It's the same with reports.

How thick is your report? How densely-packed is the text?

Will people want to pick up it up? This is so important because, if you want something done, you need the decision maker to read your report and act on your recommendations.

Therefore, when writing your report you should apply the principles of Plain English, so that 'any reasonable person can understand each sentence after only one reading.'

It should be concise, considerate and conversational. For example any jargon should be explained and any abbreviation, such as TLAs (three letter abbreviations) should, when they are first used, be written in full.

Other ways to make it easier for the reader

Break up large text with headings and subheadings.

Use generous margins and indents.

Break up large blocks of text with headings and subheadings.

Use italics or bold text for emphasis. Avoid underlining and capitals as it makes reading more difficult for some readers.

Use different fonts and font sizes for emphasis.

Use graphs, pie charts, diagrams, pictures, clip-art and so on to illustrate certain points.

Don't be too clever! People will quickly see through gimmicks.

Supporting material

If your report contains supporting data, such as research and analysis, just put a summary in the main body of the report and put the full version in the appendix for the benefit of the reader.

"Make it easy for the customer to buy"

In some reports I write, I actually go one step further than just recommending a particular option. If the report is being delivered in a hard copy, I find the specific form (e.g. an internal requisition request), complete the relevant information to support my action (e.g. to order something) and put it in the file. Then, if the decision maker has agreed with your report, it is easy for them to sign the form and the matter is closed. If they have to get the correct form etc, then they might put it off until they have the time, which may not be what you want. When possible, I make a point of collecting the completed form and pass it on to the next person.

If the report is sent as an attachment in an email, I add a P.S and refer to another attachment which is the completed form to be sent to another person or department. I also include the email address of that person or department.

These methods are risky, as you may offend the reader, so it will be a judgement on how the person is likely to react. But, if you have a good relationship, they will know what you are doing, and may actually appreciate the fact that you have saved them time by making it easy for them. Hence the term, make it easy for the person to buy.

An example of a Report

Improving our capacity to use Problem Solving

Purpose

This report outlines how we can improve the knowledge and skills of our people.

Situation

We, at ABC Trading, need to improve our position within the industry and have identified that this can be achieved by our staff being more effective at Problem Solving and Working with Others.

Problem

Our staff are not proficient in using a Problem Solving Process

Options

1 Do nothing.

Positive:
Save money. Save staff abstractions.
Negative:
Our staff do not improve their Problem Solving ability.

2 Buy in the training.

Positive:
Bring in experts, from outside the organisation, who will be effective in achieving positive learning outcomes for Problem Solving
Negative:
It will cost money and people will be away from their work.

3 Have the training delivered by our own training department.

Positive:
Low cost and the trainers know their audience.
Negative:
Our trainers do not have the expertise in Problem Solving

4 Have the training department and other suitable people trained by the external company to deliver the courses

Positive:

We increase the skills of our own workforce, cheaper to deliver to a large number of people and it is sustainable.

Negative:

Our trainers may not have the time to deliver the training,

Proposal

Option 4   Have the training department and other suitable people trained by the external company to deliver the courses.

The benefit is that, by investing in the training, our organisation can continue to train others without any further costs.

Additional section

Please find attached details of the Problem Solving Training Company, Sixth Sense and their two day Problem Solving and Partnership Course found at www.sixthsensetraining.co.uk

Appendix 4

How to deliver a Problem Solving Presentation

Decide the purpose of the presentation. You can use presentations to inform, to persuade, or to influence. What do you want to achieve? What is your purpose? Is there an issue you want the audience to understand? Do you want them:
To take action? To make a decision? To support your cause?

Know your audience

You must always keep your content relevant to your audience. You can prepare a number of quite different presentations about the same subject containing mostly the same information.

What about timing?

Control of time is very important. It makes sense to rehearse your presentation a number of times before you deliver it. Try it on relatives or friends and ask for feedback. If possible film yourself.

The importance of stating the current position

The current position is what made the presentation necessary in the first place. This must be described briefly and accurately. By the time the presentation moves into the Options phase, the audience should be in no doubt that some form of action or decision is needed.

The need for objectivity when discussing options

The audience wants the facts laid out before them in an unbiased way, so outline both the positives and the negatives.

Being able to justify your proposed option

If you tell people that something is great, be prepared to justify yourself. Your audience needs to know why it is your preferred option.

Giving your presentation

Use cue cards. Write thought triggers on each card - key words that represent a particular point to be made. The cards should be numbered, hole-punched, and held together with a tag. Only put important information on the cards.

Use of personality during the presentation

Listening to a dull, monotone voice is likely to send your audience to sleep. Let your personality shine through. Use your natural voice. There's little point in trying to change the sound of your voice. Why do it? It will only make you more nervous.

Try to relax and be yourself. When you're nervous, you'll tend to speak more quickly. However, you should try to speak a little bit slower than you normally do. This will help to ensure that everyone can hear you and, more importantly, understand you.

Use of a personal introduction

Take a deep breath, smile at your audience, and introduce yourself. The amount of detail you give in your introduction depends on the makeup of your audience. The less familiar you are with the audience, the more information you should include.

Vital Messaging

The framework for a Problem Solving Presentation is a tried and trusted method of designing and delivering presentations. However, this traditional presentation structure is designed for presentations with a fixed time slot.

But what happens when you turn up at a venue to deliver your 20 minute presentation only to find that your time slot has been reduced to 10 minutes? Or two minutes? Unfortunately, traditional presentations won't help you here. If you stick to your script, you won't reach the Vital Message – Your Proposal and/or Recommendation(s).

Therefore, have a contingency plan ready. Vital Messaging is a way of structuring your presentation so that the most important material comes **first.**

You start with the Proposal/Recommendation(s) so that you get your message across immediately. Then, time allowing, you can support your case with the important, the less important and the optional information. Hence, if you do get cut short, the Vital Message has not been lost.

This has also been described as the elevator pitch, when you meet the key person in the elevator, by chance, and you only have the time of the journey to get your message across. I strongly advise not to push the 'stop' button because, even though you would have more time, I believe the point of your message would be lost.

Appendix 5

PARTNERS Problem Solving Process

P	**Problem Definition and Partner Identification** Define the problem, under 20 words. Check for 8 common mistakes (Multiple problems, implied cause, jargon, making a statement, consequences, not being clear, limited description and aspirational). Find your partners who share your problem and/or your aims.
A	**Aim Setting** SMART Specific, measurable and time bound. Impact Scale (Eliminate it, reduce it, reduce the severity, be more efficient or persuade another to take the lead).
R	**Research and Analysis** Who is making the demand, what do they want and why? Convergent: Who, what, where, when, how long and how much? Baseline: a snap shot of the problem. Who shares your problem? Opposite: Who is not, when is it not, where is it not?
T	**Thinking Creatively** Find a time and place to think, then think differently. Look around and be inspired by others. Ensure your ideas are capable of being applied.
N	**Negotiating the Changes** Make sure you have the support of others. Set out your actions, who is leading and make a risk assessment. Monitor what you have put in place and consider sustainability.
E	**Evaluation** Was the aim met? If not, why not? What did you learn?
R	**Recognition and Reward** You need to recognise people for their help, ideas and effort.
S	**Sharing 'Good Practice'** How are you going to share what you have learnt with others, both inside and outside the organisation.